Name _____

INNOVATIONS

The Comprehensive Toddler Curriculum:

A Self-Directed Teacher's Guide

The **Comprehensive**

Todder
CURRICULUM

A Self-
Directed
Teacher's
Guide

Linda G. Miller / Kay Albrecht ●

Bulk Purchase

Gryphon House books are
available at special
discount when purchased
in bulk for special
premiums and sales
promotions as well as for
fund-raising use. Special
editions or book excerpts
also can be created to
specification. For details,
contact the Director of
Sales at the address or
phone number on this
page.

Table of Contents

Introduction

Today, you are beginning a new adventure that will support what you do in the classroom with toddlers. ***Innovations: The Comprehensive Toddler Curriculum, A Self-Directed Teacher's Guide*** is designed to provide over 40 hours of professional development for teachers using ***Innovations: The Comprehensive Toddler Curriculum***. While completing the modules in this book, you will have opportunities to explore all the different elements of curriculum that impact very young children and how they learn.

The graphic on the following page shows how comprehensive the ***Innovations*** view of curriculum is.

Developmental Tasks

Observations and Assessment

Child Development

Interactive Experiences

Teaching

Parent Participation and Involvement

Environment

Activities and Experiences

In addition to exploring the book and learning about all its different features, you will also get a chance to use the curriculum—forms, assessment instruments, activities, and ideas for making toys and materials for the classroom. By the time you complete the **Teacher's Guide**, you will have a thorough understanding of what it takes to plan and implement this exciting curriculum.

The modules in this book are designed to be completed by an individual teacher with the support (hopefully) of a mentor, supervisor, trainer, or director. Each module contains a partial Skills Checklist to assure that things you learn in training are implemented in the classroom and integrated into your teaching skills repertoire. Modules are designed to be completed in the sequence in which they appear.

We hope you enjoy your adventure both in completing this training and in enriching the lives of young children and their families. Write your name on the title page of this book, and let's get started!

Best wishes,

Linda G Miller

Kay Albrecht

Unless noted otherwise, all page numbers in this book are references to
Innovations: The Comprehensive Toddler Curriculum.

WELCOME AND PURPOSE OF TRAINING

Purpose: to introduce *Innovations: The Comprehensive Toddler Curriculum Teacher's Guide* including assumptions, reasons for teaching, and philosophy of education

TIME: APPROXIMATELY 1 HOUR

Introduction

Innovations: The Comprehensive Toddler Curriculum Teacher's Guide is designed to help teachers prepare to use *Innovations: The Comprehensive Toddler Curriculum* in the classroom. By using the *Teacher's Guide*, you will be able to learn all the many ways to use *Innovations*.

Beginning teachers will learn step-by-step about the importance of early care and education for toddlers. They will learn about basic safety issues, how to create an appropriate environment, how young children learn, and how to include parents in the lives of their children at school. Experienced teachers will have opportunities to learn about new curriculum ideas and to understand concepts of child development. All teachers will be challenged to perfect their skills of interaction, curriculum development, observation, documentation, and assessment.

Assumptions

This teacher-training guide is based on the following assumptions:
* *All teachers need initial, as well as on-going training—no matter what their level of formal education is.* Life-long learning is important for everyone, especially teachers. New research in the area of child development provides insight into how young children grow and learn.
* *Parents are their children's first and most important teachers.* Parents have a stronger and more lasting effect on their children than anyone or anything else. Early attachment determines how safe a child feels, how he feels about himself, and how he relates to others.
* *In addition to their parents, children's teachers are of primary importance in their young lives.* A toddler's teacher is a significant adult in terms of attachment and interaction, facilitating emotional and social development. Additionally, teachers have a direct influence on a child's language development through quality interactions.
* *Children's initial experiences with adults are critical in determining how they will relate to others, how they will feel about themselves, and how they will perform academically.* When children have their needs met promptly (when an adult responds to crying in a timely and sensitive manner), they cry less

often. Young children learn that their needs will be met and that the world is a safe place to be.

* All children deserve to be in an environment where they are safe, loved, and learning. Early care and education are crucial for all young children. The early years are learning years—especially important for early brain development. Learning windows open, creating an opportunity to stimulate brain development. During these critical periods, children are extremely sensitive to stimulation from interactions and experiences.

* Being involved in the lives of young children and their families through teaching is an enriching and stimulating experience. Because "We are shaped and fashioned by what we love" (Goethe), being involved in the lives of young children and their families can be very special and fulfilling.

Why Teach?

Use the space below to explain why you want to teach toddlers.

What are your beliefs about how you should educate very young children?

_____   _____

Teacher Completing Training Module   Date
(please sign and date)

Congratulations! You have completed Module 1 of 38 in the **Teacher's Guide**.

GET ACQUAINTED WITH INNOVATIONS: THE COMPREHENSIVE TODDLER CURRICULUM

Purpose: to become familiar with *Innovations: The Comprehensive Toddler Curriculum*

TIME: APPROXIMATELY 1 HOUR

During this module, you will have an opportunity to get to know how *Innovations: The Comprehensive Toddler Curriculum* is put together. (You might find it helpful to create tabs, so you can turn quickly to the different sections.)

Chapter 1—Getting Started (pages 17-36) provides an overview to the entire book. Read the introduction and then find the following sections, which show a variety of what the book offers. Use the Table of Contents (pages 7-12) and the Index (pages 585-608) to find the page numbers.

READ THIS

Page Number	Book Section
_____	Chapter 2—Transitioning to School
_____	Possibilities Plan: Space
_____	Possibilities Plan: Water
_____	Chapter 5—Communicating with Parents, Teachers, and Friends
_____	Songs, Poems, Rhymes, and Fingerplays
_____	Blank Forms
_____	Parent Postcards

You will have additional opportunities to get to know the book as you continue with your training.

_____   _____

Teacher Completing Training Module   Date
(please sign and date)

Congratulations! You have completed Module 2 of 38 in the *Teacher's Guide*.

PERSONAL GOALS FOR TRAINING IN TEACHER'S GUIDE

Purpose: to create personal training goals, including goals related to curriculum planning, goals related to observation and assessment, and goals related to child development/specific behaviors

TIME: APPROXIMATELY 1 HOUR

Innovations: The Comprehensive Toddler Curriculum is unique in that it views curriculum in a very broad sense. During your training, you will learn about all the following aspects of curriculum that have an impact on toddlers.

Developmental Tasks

Observations and Assessment

Child Development

Interactive Experiences

Teaching

Parent Participation and Involvement

Environment

Activities and Experiences

As a teacher, it is important for you to set goals. This module will give you an opportunity to do so in specific areas related to your **Innovations** training. You may find it helpful to look back through Chapter 1—Getting Started (pages 17-36) as you write your goals.

My training goal for activities and experiences is to:
(for example, learn five new activities in each Possibilities area, add sensory/art activities to my curriculum planning, or try one project with toddlers)

My curriculum planning goal is to:
(for example, add webbing to the planning process I use, or invite parents to participate in webbing as part of my curriculum planning)

My observation and assessment goal is to:
(for example, complete one observation on each child each week, or use observations to assess children's development)

My child development/child behavior goal is to:
(for example, understand the behaviors associated with different developmental ages and stages, or help parents understand children's ages and stages and the impact of age and stage on parenting)

Skills Checklist

If you are currently in the classroom, use the complete list on page 95 of this book as a frequent skills checklist to confirm that you are developing your teaching skills repertoire. You may either fill out the Skills Checklist yourself or ask a teacher to observe you and complete the Skills Checklist for you (peer evaluation). If you are unfamiliar with an item, read about it in the book or talk with your mentor or trainer. The following is an abbreviated checklist related to this module.

_____Parents and toddlers are greeted warmly. (see pages 45-46)
_____Toys and equipment are disinfected. (see pages 303, 404-405)
_____Diapering procedures are followed. (see pages 385-386)
_____Quality interactions occur during the day. (see pages 294-295)
_____Safety precautions are followed in the classroom (for example, attendance taken, toddlers never left alone, chokeable items eliminated, toys and materials regularly checked for safety). (see page 385)

All teachers need someone to talk with and discuss issues concerning the classroom. Individuals can complete this teacher's guide independently, but interaction with a mentor or trainer will make this a more powerful professional experience. Identify the person you will use as a resource in the space below. Consider asking a more experienced teacher, a supervisor, an education professor, a community college teacher, a director, or a consultant from a resource and referral agency.

My mentor or trainer is _____

_____   _____

Teacher Completing Training Module   Date
(please sign and date)

Congratulations! You have completed Module 3 of 38 in the **Teacher's Guide**.

DEVELOPMENTAL TASKS

Purpose: to learn about the developmental tasks included in
Innovations: The Comprehensive Toddler Curriculum, how they differ
from other developmental lists, and how to use them while observing
toddlers

TIME: APPROXIMATELY 1 HOUR

Developmental tasks are the very large developmental challenges that
children experience as they learn and grow. Most curriculum models focus on
the sequence of emerging development. However, **Innovations** focuses on how
to encourage, facilitate, and stimulate development. It is interactional,
viewing development as the complex interplay between the child and the
world. Major interactional tasks are identified and used to construct
developmentally appropriate approaches to early education of toddlers.
Developmental tasks in *Innovations: The Comprehensive Toddler Curriculum*
are loosely sequential from Chapter 2 through Chapter 7.

The developmental tasks of this curriculum are Transitioning to School
(Chapter 2—page 37); Making Friends (Chapter 3—page 121); Exploring
Roles (Chapter 4—page 215); Communicating with Parents, Teachers, and
Friends (Chapter 5—page 281); Problem Solving (Chapter 6—page 367);
and Expressing Feelings with Parents, Teachers, and Friends (Chapter 7—
page 453).

READ THIS

Take some time to read about the different developmental tasks in
Innovations: The Comprehensive Toddler Curriculum.

Because developmental tasks are very broad in nature, they often encompass
several, or even all of the components of child development (physical,
intellectual, emotional, and social). Some people recall these components of
development by remembering PIES.

The PIES of Child Development

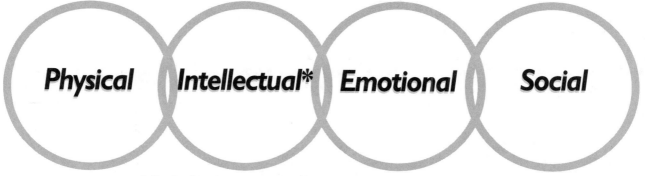

Physical   **Intellectual***   **Emotional**   **Social**

* Includes language and cognition

Read the skills in the developmental task of Making Friends (from Chapter 3, page 123). Label the different boxes as Physical (P), Intellectual (I), Emotional (E), or Social (S). (You will see lots of overlap. The younger the child, the more overlap we see in the domains.)

Toddler (18-36 months) Assessment

Task: Making Friends

	18-24 months	24-30 months	30-36 months
MF1	a. Calms self with verbal support from adults and transitional objects.	b. Calms self with verbal support from adults; may look for transitional objects to help with the calm-down process after verbal support is provided. Frequency of emotional outburst begins to diminish.	c. Calms self with only verbal support. Use of transitional objects begins to decline except at bedtime and when recovering from intense emotional outbursts.
MF2	a Goes to mirror to look at self; makes faces and shows emotions like laughing, crying, and so on.	b. Calls own name when looking at photographs or in the mirror.	c. Calls names of friends in photographs or in the mirror.
MF3	a. Develops preferences for types of play and types of toys.	b. Develops play themes that are repeated again and again (such as mommy or firefighter).	c. Begins exploration of a wider range of play themes. Themes often come from new experiences.
MF4	a. Perfects gross motor skills such as running, climbing, and riding push toys. Fine motor skills with manipulatives (simple puzzles, Duplos, and so on) are emerging.	b. Likes physical challenges such as running fast, jumping high, and going up and down stairs. Plays with preferred manipulatives for increasing periods of time.	c. Competently exhibits a wide range of physical skills. Begins to be interested in practicing skills such as throwing a ball, riding a tricycle, or completing a puzzle.
MF5	a. Play may be onlooker, solitary, or parallel in nature.	b. Play is predominantly parallel in nature.	c. Exhibits associative play with familiar play partners.
MF6	a. Exhibits symbolic play.	b. Practices and explores a wide variety of symbolic play themes and roles.	
MF7	a. Objects to strangers' presence; clings, cries, and seeks support when strangers are around.	b. Objection to strangers begins to diminish; may still be wary of strangers or new situations.	c. Is able to venture into strange or new situations if prepared in advance and supported by adults.
MF8	a. Uses single words to indicate needs and wants such as "muk" for "I want milk," or "bye bye" for "Let's go bye bye."	b. Uses phrases and 2- to 3-word sentences to indicate needs and wants.	c. Uses 4- to 6-word sentences to indicate needs and wants.

	18-24 months	24-30 months		30-36 months
MF9	a. Connects emotions with behaviors; uses language to express these connections.	b. Uses emotional ideas in play.	c. Elaborates on emotional ideas and understanding to play with objects.	d. Begins emotional thinking; begins to understand emotional cause-and-effect relationships.

	18-24 months	24-30 months	30-36 months
MF10	a. Takes turns with toys and materials with adult support and facilitation.	b. Takes turns with toys and materials with friend, sometimes without adult support.	
MF11	a. Experiments with behavior that accomplishes a goal; may bite, pinch, poke, scratch, push, and so on while trying to make things happen.	b. Begins to anticipate what might happen when actions are taken; chooses to make things happen if outcomes are desirable (for example, trade toys with a friend who will stay and play), and resists taking action if outcomes are undesirable (for example, teacher putting markers away if child chews on the tips).	

Skills Checklist

If you are currently in the classroom, use the complete list on page 95 of this book as a frequent skills checklist to confirm that you are developing your teaching skills repertoire. You may either fill out the Skills Checklist yourself or ask a teacher to observe you and complete the Skills Checklist for you (peer evaluation). If you are unfamiliar with an item, read about it in the book or talk with your mentor or trainer. The following is an abbreviated checklist related to this module.

_____Toys and equipment are disinfected. (see pages 303, 404-405)
_____Diapering procedures are followed. (see pages 385-386)
_____Quality interactions occur during the day. (see pages 294-295)
_____Safety precautions are followed in the classroom (for example, attendance taken, toddlers never left alone, chokeable items eliminated, toys and materials examined for safety). (see page 385)
_____Teacher observes toddlers regularly during the day. (see pages 18-21)

_____   _____

Teacher Completing Training Module   Date
(please sign and date)

Congratulations! You have completed Module 4 of 38 in the **Teacher's Guide**.

INNOVATIONS IN OBSERVATION/ASSESSMENT

Purpose: to use a developmental continuum for observation and assessment

TIME: APPROXIMATELY 1½ HOURS

The three major goals for observation and assessment are:

Goal 1 To help teachers and parents see children as individuals who have unique skills

Goal 2 To insure developmentally appropriate practice

Goal 3 To guide curriculum development that is sensitive to children's emerging skills, but does not frustrate or overstimulate

This curriculum relies on nonstandardized assessment techniques including:

1. systematic observation
2. anecdotal notes
3. normative checklist

READ THIS ➤

Read the task continuum for each of the developmental tasks. These are located in sections called Innovations in Observation/Assessment (pages 38-39, 122-123, 217, 282-283, 368-369, 454-455). Look at the completed assessment on pages 114-121 of this book to see one possible way to use the continuum for developmental assessment.

Then spend time observing one toddler. Perform the following assessment by making three different observations of 5-10 minutes each. Do not mark a subtask unless you observe it.

You will notice that a child may display the behaviors in the box designated for 18-24 months in one subtask, while the same child displays the behaviors in the box designated for 24-30 months on another subtask. This shows the unevenness of development that is typical throughout childhood. Also, notice that you were not able to mark everything. Children do not learn in a straight line. Development is sporadic in nature and proceeds in fits and starts.

To use the results of the assessment, identify a subtask that you did not mark. Next plan an activity (from pages 71-120) or an experience (pages 45-46) that will make it possible for you to observe and assess that subtask.

Which activity or experience did you choose?

What did you observe?

Keep a copy of the assessment (page 39) on a clipboard in your classroom, so you can observe and assess regularly.

Skills Checklist

If you are currently in the classroom, use the complete list on page 95 of this book as a frequent skills checklist to confirm that you are developing your teaching skills repertoire. You may either fill out the Skills Checklist yourself or ask a teacher to observe you and complete the Skills Checklist for you (peer evaluation). If you are unfamiliar with an item, read about it in the book or talk with your mentor or trainer. The following is an abbreviated checklist related to this module.

_____Diapering procedures are followed. (see pages 385-386)

_____Quality interactions occur during the day. (see pages 294-295)

_____Safety precautions are followed in the classroom (for example, attendance taken, toddlers never left alone, chokeable items eliminated, toys and materials examined for safety). (see page 385)

_____Teacher observes toddlers regularly during the day. (see pages 18-21)

_____Assessment materials are readily available in the classroom (clipboard, pen, forms). (see page 21)

_____   _____

Teacher Completing Training Module   Date
(please sign and date)

Congratulations! You have completed Module 5 of 38 in the **Teacher's Guide**.

MODULE 6

INNOVATIONS IN CHILD DEVELOPMENT

Purpose: to identify the relationship between toddler behaviors and child development principles

TIME: APPROXIMATELY 1½ HOURS

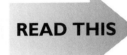

Each chapter includes a section explaining the underlying theory or child development principles, best practices, or content knowledge leading to specific developmental tasks. Child development is under the heading Innovations in Child Development (pages 40-45, 124-127, 218-221, 284-294, 370-373, 456-457). These sections are helpful to teachers as they support children's growth and development. Topics include separation anxiety, primary teaching, literacy development, toddler personalities, and social development theories. Innovations in Child Development will show you "why" children behave in different ways.

Often teachers view toddler behaviors in isolation. However, toddlers have their particular characteristics because of underlying child development principles. The following chart shows the relationship between some common "challenges" in the classroom and the child development topics related to them.

Classroom Challenges	Child Development Topics
Biting	Prosocial behavior (pages 136-139)
Aggression	Emotional behavior (pages 133-135)
Temper tantrums	Attachment theory (pages 466-467)
Discipline problems	Guidance and discipline (pages 43-45)

Choose a classroom challenge with which you need help or one in which you are interested. Read the section referenced that deals with the appropriate child development topic.

How can knowing about child development help with the classroom challenge you chose?

Skills Checklist

If you are currently in the classroom, use the complete list on page 95 of this book as a frequent skills checklist to confirm that you are developing your teaching skills repertoire. You may either fill out the Skills Checklist yourself or ask a teacher to observe you and complete the Skills Checklist for you (peer evaluation). If you are unfamiliar with an item, read about it in the book or talk with your mentor or trainer. The following is an abbreviated checklist related to this module.

_____Quality interactions occur during the day. (see pages 294-295)

_____Safety precautions are followed in the classroom (for example, attendance taken, toddlers never left alone, chokeable items eliminated, toys and materials examined for safety). (see page 385)

_____Teacher observes toddlers regularly during the day. (see pages 18-21)

_____Assessment materials are readily available in the classroom (clipboard, pen, forms). (see page 21)

_____Teacher explores and discovers the relationship between behavior and child development principles. (see pages 40-45)

_____   _____

Teacher Completing Training Module   Date
(please sign and date)

Congratulations! You have completed Module 6 of 38 in the **Teacher's Guide**.

INNOVATIONS IN INTERACTIVE EXPERIENCES

Purpose: to learn how to plan and use routine times to provide quality interactions for toddlers

TIME: APPROXIMATELY 1 HOUR

This curriculum advocates thinking about and planning for everything that can, by the nature of the setting (school vs. home), contribute to a child's development and the teacher's relationship with the child and family.

The sections Innovations in Interactive Experiences are a necessary part of the curriculum plan and include types of experiences that you, as the teacher, must observe, plan, support, and provide.

READ THIS →

Much of the day for toddlers and their teachers is spent in routine care (diapering, feeding, napping). So, when thinking about time for quality interactions between toddlers and adults, we might think "when?" The answer to that question is during routine times. Read the following list of experiences (from Chapter 2, page 46). Similar lists of experiences are included in each chapter under Innovations in Interactive Experiences (pages 45-46, 127-128, 221, 294-295, 373, 457-458).

Life's minutiae build to create experiences. Toddler teachers must be attuned to these everyday, yet important, experiences. They are truly the foundation upon which crucial skills and abilities grow. Think about the following list of experiences and make sure that the classroom reflects many of them.

☐ Prepare children for transitions. Until they have a great deal more experience with change, toddlers will struggle each time there is a transition. Talk to toddlers about what is going to happen to them next, and tell them what is going on. Give 5-minute, then 3-minute, then 1-minute reminders that change is about to occur.

☐ Leave a written record for the teacher who is arriving. This can take the form of a Communication Sheet (see page 537 in the Appendix) or a notebook with notes about what the child might need next. Written records do not rely on verbal exchanges that may get lost in the midst of the transition.

☐ Watch the tone of your voice and your nonverbal cues during interactions. Congruence between what you say and the way you say it, and what you do and the way you do it is communication. This is extremely important when you "tire" of toddler behaviors, such as when you leave and you know the child will get upset and cry. If you indicate that the child's feelings are not important, either intentionally or unintentionally, the message the child gets is that her feelings don't matter.

☐ Support children as they experience new stimuli. When new things are happening in the school environment, toddlers need support in taking in the new stimuli. Sometimes this support is preparatory, such as warning a child that the fire alarm is going to go off in a minute and make a loud noise, or reminding children that you are going to ask them to stop what they are doing and go outside.

☐ Provide support physically as well as visually when children experience new things. Regardless of temperament, children benefit from being close to someone that they trust while new experiences are being offered. Get down on children's eye level, hold them close, look where they look, and follow the child's lead. When physical support is no longer needed, visually support the child with eye contact and nonverbal cues such as smiling and nodding your head.

By planning for quality interactions, you can use all the time during the day to support children's growth and development.

Look in the Possibilities Plan: Me and My Body (pages 71-92) and Possibilities Plan: My Family (pages 93-120) to see what specific activities are appropriate to ensure that the experiences occur during the day. Write the title of the activities under the experience they match.

READ THIS

Skills Checklist

If you are currently in the classroom, use the complete list on page 95 of this book as a frequent skills checklist to confirm that you are developing your teaching skills repertoire. You may either fill out the Skills Checklist yourself or ask a teacher to observe you and complete the Skills Checklist for you (peer evaluation). If you are unfamiliar with an item, read about it in the book or talk with your mentor or trainer. The following is an abbreviated checklist related to this module.

_____Safety precautions are followed in the classroom (for example, attendance taken, toddlers never left alone, chokeable items eliminated, toys and materials examined for safety). (see page 385)
_____Teacher observes toddlers regularly during the day. (see pages 18-21)
_____Assessment materials are readily available in the classroom (clipboard, pen, forms). (see page 21)
_____Teacher explores and discovers the relationship between behavior and child development principles. (see pages 40-45)
_____Teacher uses routine times to provide individual quality interactions for toddlers. (see page 53)

_____   _____

Teacher Completing Training Module   Date
(please sign and date)

Congratulations! You have completed Module 7 of 38 in the **Teacher's Guide**.

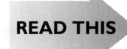
INNOVATIONS IN TEACHING

8

Purpose: to support the development of teacher competencies by using the Innovations in Teaching sections in the chapters

TIME: APPROXIMATELY I HOUR

READ THIS

Each chapter contains a section called Innovations in Teaching (pages 47-57, 128-141, 222-227, 295-308, 374-390, 459-474). In these sections, you learn about issues that are important in the classroom. Also included in the section is a checklist entitled Teacher Competencies that you can use to evaluate yourself. You may also use the checklist for peer evaluation or evaluation by a mentor or trainer. Resources for Teachers contains additional reading for teachers.

Read Innovations in Teaching in Chapter 2 (pages 47-57) and Temperament in Toddlers (pages 43-45). Then complete the following activity. Observe one child in your classroom or in another available classroom. Mark each item on the continuum to the right. Behaviors are described on a continuum from low to high.

Toddler Temperament Chart

Nine character traits have been identified to gauge a child's temperament and to help determine the most effective method of caring for each child:

1) activity level

2) regularity of biological rhythms
    (sleeping, eating, and elimination)

3) approach/withdrawal tendencies

4) mood

5) intensity of reaction

6) adaptability

7) sensitivity to light, touch, taste,
    sound, and sights

8) distractibility

9) persistence

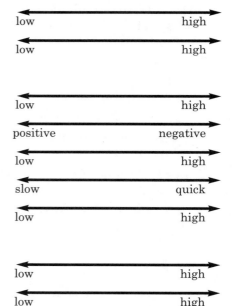

(Use the results to determine if the child is primarily flexible, fearful, or feisty. Discuss your findings with your mentor or trainer.)

The Teacher Competencies in each chapter are useful for self-evaluation or evaluation by a mentor or trainer. Use the list of Teacher Competencies from Chapter 2 below to rate yourself on behaviors that support children as they transition to school. Mark the box labeled sometimes, usually, or always for each competency.

Teacher Competencies to Support Transitioning to School

Sometimes	Usually	Always	
☐	☐	☐	Looks up, acknowledges, and greets children and parents as they arrive in the classroom.
☐	☐	☐	Facilitates child's entry into the classroom and separation from parents as they leave.
☐	☐	☐	Accepts and respects each child as she is. Indicates this respect by talking about what is going to happen and waiting for indications of wants or needs before responding.
☐	☐	☐	Shows an awareness of each child's temperament and level of development.
☐	☐	☐	Responds quickly to children who need attention.
☐	☐	☐	Allows children to follow their own schedules; changes with the children as schedules fluctuate. Is an alert observer of each child in the classroom.
☐	☐	☐	Uses routines of eating, resting, and diapering as opportunities to maximize reciprocal interactions.
☐	☐	☐	Monitors children's general comfort and health (for example, warmth, dryness, noses wiped, wet clothes changed, and so on).
☐	☐	☐	Invests in quality time with infants throughout the day during routines and stimulation activities.
☐	☐	☐	Uses floor time to build relationships with children.
☐	☐	☐	Maintains a positive, pleasant attitude toward parents; thinks in terms of creating a partnership to support the child.
☐	☐	☐	Communicates regularly with parents about the child's experience at school; uses a variety of techniques to keep communication flowing freely.
☐	☐	☐	Plans, implements, and evaluates regular parent participation experiences, parent/teacher conferences, and parent education experiences.
☐	☐	☐	Supports children's developing awareness by talking about families, displaying families' photographs, and celebrating accomplishments.
☐	☐	☐	Uses books, pictures, and stories to help children identify with events that occur in the world of the family and the school.

Select one competency you feel needs improvement. Make a plan to improve it and discuss your plan with your mentor.

Skills Checklist

If you are currently in the classroom, use the complete list on page 95 of this book as a frequent skills checklist to confirm that you are developing your teaching skills repertoire. You may either fill out the Skills Checklist yourself or ask a teacher to observe you and complete the Skills Checklist for you (peer evaluation). If you are unfamiliar with an item, read about it in the book or talk with your mentor or trainer. The following is an abbreviated checklist related to this module.

_____Teacher observes toddlers regularly during the day. (see pages 18-21)

_____Assessment materials are readily available in the classroom (clipboard, pen, forms). (see page 21)

_____Teacher explores and discovers the relationship between behavior and child development principles. (see pages 40-45)

_____Teacher uses routine times to provide individual quality interactions for toddlers. (see page 53)

_____Teacher uses reflection to assess and improve teaching competencies. (see page 23)

_____   _____

Teacher Completing Training Module   Date
(please sign and date)

Congratulations! You have completed Module 8 of 38 in the **Teacher's Guide**.

INNOVATIONS IN PARENT PARTNERSHIPS

Purpose: to create partnerships between teachers and parents

TIME: APPROXIMATELY 1 HOUR

Parents, more than any other person, influence the children in your care. No matter how long toddlers are in group care during the day, their parents are still their primary educators and their child's first and most important teachers. By keeping parents informed, listening to their concerns, and welcoming them to participate in their child's experiences at school, you are able to form partnerships to strengthen families and support children's learning.

Innovations: The Comprehensive Toddler Curriculum provides many different ways to develop partnerships with parents and encourage them to participate in their child's life at school. Each chapter includes a section called Innovations in Parent Partnerships that makes suggestions for school-initiated possibilities (such as collecting materials to be made into toys for the classroom), parent participation activities (such as invitations for parents to come to a parent meeting), parent postcards (which include topics to assist parents in understanding and supporting their child's growth and development), and additional resources for parents (pages 58-67, 142-157, 227-230, 308-319, 391-402, 474-484). In addition to all these options, you also can find ideas on how to involve parents in activities and additional postcards in all the different Possibilities Plans. For example, in Possibilities Plan: Me and My Body, see the Parent Participation Possibilities section on pages 87-89 for participation ideas and postcards.

READ THIS

Parental involvement helps everyone. Parents have a higher rate of satisfaction with their child's teacher and their child's school when they are involved. Toddlers benefit when partnerships are formed between the teacher and the parent. And the teacher benefits from the insight and understanding of the family and the child, creating the best possible situation to support the child in the classroom.

Choose an activity in Chapter 2 to encourage parents to be involved. Write the activity you chose below.

Implement the activity. Then, explain how it worked.

How will you change the activity if you use it again?

Reflecting on the success of chosen parent participation activities allows teachers to modify future plans based on the information and insight gained.

Skills Checklist

If you are currently in the classroom, use the complete list on page 95 of this book as a frequent skills checklist to confirm that you are developing your teaching skills repertoire. You may either fill out the Skills Checklist yourself or ask a teacher to observe you and complete the Skills Checklist for you (peer evaluation). If you are unfamiliar with an item, read about it in the book or talk with your mentor or trainer. The following is an abbreviated checklist related to this module.

_____Assessment materials are readily available in the classroom (clipboard, pen, forms). (see page 21)

_____Teacher explores and discovers the relationship between behavior and child development principles. (see pages 40-45)

_____Teacher uses routine times to provide individual, child-focused, quality interactions for toddlers. (see page 53)

_____Teacher uses reflection to assess and improve teaching competencies. (see page 23)

_____Teacher supports partnerships with parents through planning and implementing regular parent participation opportunities. (see page 24)

_____Teacher modifies parent participation choices as a result of reflection about the success of planned activities.

_____   _____

Teacher Completing Training Module   Date
(please sign and date)

Congratulations! You have completed Module 9 of 38 in the **Teacher's Guide**.

INNESTON INNOVATIONS IN ENVIRONMENTS

Purpose: to evaluate important classroom elements that make up the environment

TIME: APPROXIMATELY 1 HOUR

Every classroom has an unusual "extra" teacher. That teacher is the environment. Children learn through the active exploration of their surroundings, so you must plan an appropriate learning environment for the toddlers in your care. Children in full-day programs have to "live" in their school settings (Greenman and Stonehouse, 1996).
Because of this, stimulation activities must be balanced across the important dimensions of activity (quiet or active), location (indoor or outdoor), and initiator (child-initiated or adult-initiated) (Bredekamp, 1997; National Academy of Early Childhood Programs, 1991). Include items from Innovations in Environment on the possibilities plan to add to the environment. Read page 70 for things to consider when choosing furniture and equipment.

Teachers have the following responsibilities for the environment:

* ***Creating the Environment***—Teachers use their knowledge of what a classroom needs to determine room arrangement and the organization of materials.

* ***Maintaining the Environment***—Teachers keep the environment safe by inspecting toys and the classroom for problems. Teachers fix or discard broken toys or toys with missing pieces, and they routinely disinfect toys and surfaces.

* ***Refreshing the Environment***—Teachers plan for different experiences by adding a variety of different materials and taking away some of the old materials. A balance between novel toys, materials, and experiences and familiar toys, materials, and experiences is achieved.

Use the checklist on the following page to evaluate your classroom. Place a check to indicate if you agree, somewhat agree, or disagree.

Classroom Evaluation

Date _____

	Agree	Somewhat Agree	Disagree
Elements are in place that create a sense of calm in the classroom.	☐	☐	☐
Sufficient soft elements help make the environment more home-like.	☐	☐	☐
Appropriate places are provided for toddlers' things in the classroom.	☐	☐	☐
The classroom is a predictable environment that includes novel and interesting things.	☐	☐	☐
The classroom includes places to be alone that do not sacrifice visual supervision.	☐	☐	☐
The classroom includes opportunities for different perspectives (platform, windows, doors).	☐	☐	☐
The classroom includes places to climb.	☐	☐	☐
Materials and toys are stored on low shelves in clear labeled containers.	☐	☐	☐
Stimulation in the classroom can be decreased and increased (light, music, nature sounds).	☐	☐	☐

Next, use the evaluation to determine a goal you have for improving your classroom. Write it below (for example, create places for each toddler to put his or her things, or add some soft elements such as pillows or carpets to the environment).

Skills Checklist

If you are currently in the classroom, use the complete list on page 95 of this book as a frequent skills checklist to confirm that you are developing your teaching skills repertoire. You may either fill out the Skills Checklist yourself or ask a teacher to observe you and complete the Skills Checklist for you (peer evaluation). If you are unfamiliar with an item, read about it in the book or talk with your mentor or trainer. The following is an abbreviated checklist related to this module.

_____Teacher explores and discovers the relationship between behavior and child development principles. (see pages 40-45)

_____Teacher uses routine times to provide individual quality interactions for toddlers. (see page 53)

_____Teacher uses reflection to assess and improve teaching competencies. (see page 23)

_____Teacher supports partnerships with parents through planning and implementing regular parent participation opportunities. (see page 24)

_____Teacher creates, maintains, and refreshes appropriate classroom environment. (see pages 67-69)

_____   _____

Teacher Completing Training Module   Date
(please sign and date)

Congratulations! You have completed Module 10 of 38 in the **_Teacher's Guide_**.

MODULE 11

ACTIVITIES AND EXPERIENCES

Purpose: to recognize the different types of possibilities (activities and experiences) in the classroom

TIME: APPROXIMATELY 1½ HOURS

Activities and experiences are an important aspect of curriculum. Innovations in Interactive Experiences, a section that appears in each chapter, provides important experiences that you can provide for toddlers throughout the day.

READ THIS →

Additionally, you can find activities throughout the Possibilities sections of the book (Possibilities Plan: Me and My Body, pages 71-92; Possibilities Plan: My Family, pages 93-120; Possibilities Plan: My Neighborhood, pages 163-190; Possibilities Plan: Fruits and Vegetables, pages 191-214; Possibilities Plan: Space, pages 235-260; Possibilities Plan: Sky, pages 261-280; Possibilities Plan: Big Animals, pages 323-346; Possibilities Plan: Little Animals, pages 347-366; Possibilities Plan: Construction, pages 407-428; Possibilities Plan: Wheels, pages 429-452; Possibilities Plan: Storybook Characters, pages 487-506; and Possibilities Plan: Water, pages 507-533). Possibilities Plans are included in and related to each of the six developmental tasks.

Copy the icons on the following page and cut them out. (Enlarge the icons, if necessary.) Tape them to the places in the room where you find toys and materials of that type. For example, tape the Dramatic Possibilities icon to the place in the room where you keep dolls and dishes.

After you tape the icon signs around the room, look to see if you used all of them. For example, if you do not have a CD player and CD's, you probably did not use the Music icon. List below the icons that you did not use:

Now, look to see if you need additional icons. If so, make another copy, cut out the icons, and again tape them to the places in the room where you find toys and materials of that type. List the icons that you used more than once:

What did you learn from this exercise? What will you need to consider in the future as you plan, prepare, and refresh the environment?

Skills Checklist

If you are currently in the classroom, use the complete list on page 95 of this book as a frequent skills checklist to confirm that you are developing your teaching skills repertoire. You may either fill out the Skills Checklist yourself or ask a teacher to observe you and complete the Skills Checklist for you (peer evaluation). If you are unfamiliar with an item, read about it in the book or talk with your mentor or trainer. The following is an abbreviated checklist related to this module.

_____Teacher uses routine times to provide individual quality interactions for toddlers. (see page 53)

_____Teacher uses reflection to assess and improve teaching competencies. (see page 23)

_____Teacher supports partnerships with parents through planning and implementing regular parent participation opportunities. (see page 24)

_____Teacher creates, maintains, and refreshes appropriate classroom environment. (see pages 67-69)

_____Classroom contains experiences and activities that reflect a wide variety of possibilities for children in the classroom. (see pages 24-29)

_____   _____

Teacher Completing Training Module   Date
(please sign and date)

Congratulations! You have completed Module 11 of 38 in the **Teacher's Guide**.

WEBBING

Purpose: to learn about webbing and to practice webbing techniques for curriculum planning

TIME: APPROXIMATELY 1 HOUR

Webbing is a method used to create many different possibilities for activities and experiences and create a picture of the direction in which children's learning might proceed. Through webs, you can provide divergent ideas and identify appropriate knowledge and skills for young children. Each Possibilities Plan starts with a curriculum web. Use these webs as you plan for activities and experiences in your classroom, or make your own webs.

Look at the webs that begin each Possibilities Plan (pages 71, 93, 163, 191, 235, 261, 323, 347, 407, 429, 487, 507). Glance through the activities following the webs to see how they relate.

READ THIS

Create a web of your own for one of the following new topics:

Baby Animals
Lights
Birds and Butterflies
Stripes and Dots

Draw your web here.

Skills Checklist

If you are currently in the classroom, use the complete list on page 95 of this book as a frequent skills checklist to confirm that you are developing your teaching skills repertoire. You may either fill out the Skills Checklist yourself or ask a teacher to observe you and complete the Skills Checklist for you (peer evaluation). If you are unfamiliar with an item, read about it in the book or talk with your mentor or trainer. The following is an abbreviated checklist related to this module.

_____Teacher uses reflection to assess and improve teaching competencies. (see page 23)

_____Teacher supports partnerships with parents through planning and implementing regular parent participation opportunities. (see page 24)

_____Teacher creates, maintains, and refreshes appropriate classroom environment. (see pages 67-69)

_____Classroom contains experiences and activities that reflect a wide variety of possibilities for children in the classroom. (see pages 24-29)

_____Teacher uses webbing as a technique to support emergent curriculum. (see page 25)

_____   _____

Teacher Completing Training Module   Date
(please sign and date)

Congratulations! You have completed Module 12 of 38 in the **Teacher's Guide**.

PLANNING PAGES

Purpose: to practice using planning pages for Possibilities Plans

TIME: APPROXIMATELY 1 HOUR

Each Possibilities Plan begins with planning pages. Glance through all the planning pages included in the book.

Possibilities Plan	Page Numbers for Planning Pages
Me and My Body	pages 72-73
My Family	pages 94-95
My Neighborhood	pages 164-165
Fruits and Vegetables	pages 192-193
Space	pages 236-237
Sky	pages 262-263
Big Animals	pages 324-325
Little Animals	pages 348-349
Construction	pages 408-409
Wheels	pages 430-431
Storybook Characters	pages 488-489
Water	pages 508-509

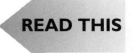

READ THIS

Planning pages are a summary of the titles of the activities and materials with their page references. Often when you are just trying to get some new ideas, you can use the planning pages to glance through and quickly get the activities.

Turn back to one of the Possibilities Plans. Choose two different activities, turn to the pages listed, and read how to do them. Which activities did you choose?

What appealed to you about these particular activities?

Skills Checklist

If you are currently in the classroom, use the complete list on page 95 of this book as a frequent skills checklist to confirm that you are developing your teaching skills repertoire. You may either fill out the Skills Checklist yourself or ask a teacher to observe you and complete the Skills Checklist for you (peer evaluation). If you are unfamiliar with an item, read about it in the book or talk with your mentor or trainer. The following is an abbreviated checklist related to this module.

_____Teacher uses reflection to assess and improve teaching competencies. (see page 23)

_____Teacher supports partnerships with parents through planning and implementing regular parent participation opportunities. (see page 24)

_____Teacher creates, maintains, and refreshes appropriate classroom environment. (see pages 67-69)

_____Classroom contains experiences and activities that reflect a wide variety of possibilities for children in the classroom. (see pages 24-29)

_____Teacher uses webbing as a technique to support emergent curriculum. (see page 25)

_____   _____

Teacher Completing Training Module   Date
(please sign and date)

Congratulations! You have completed Module 13 of 38 in the **Teacher's Guide**.

POSSIBILITIES

Purpose: to explore the different types of possibilities in the book and to determine the possibilities and materials needed for your classroom

TIME: APPROXIMATELY 1 HOUR

Read about the different possibilities for the toddler room in Possibilities Plans in Chapter 1: Getting Started (pages 24-29). Possibilities Plans contain the following elements:

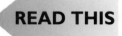

1. Webs (example, page 71)
2. Planning Pages (example, pages 72-73)
3. Dramatic Possibilities (example, pages 74-75)
4. Sensory and Art Possibilities (example, pages 75-77)
5. Curiosity Possibilities (example, pages 77-78)
6. Construction Possibilities (example, page 79)
7 . Literacy Possibilities (example, pages 79-81)
8 . Music Possibilities (example, pages 81-83)
9 . Movement Possibilities (example, pages 83-84)
10. Outdoor Possibilities (example, pages 84-86)
11. Project Possibilities (example, pages 86-87)
12. Parent Participation Possibilities (example, page 87)
13. Concepts Learned (example, page 90)
14. Resources (example, pages 90-92)
> Prop Boxes
> Picture File/Vocabulary
> Books
> Rhymes/Fingerplays
> Music/Songs
15. Toys and Materials (gathered and bought) (example, page 92)

Look back at Module 11. What types of possibilities do you have missing in your classroom? Below, write a goal you have for including materials that currently are not in your room. Create a "wish list" for materials needed for your classroom.

Goal for adding Possibilities: (for example, add sensory, music, and dramatic play toys and materials to the classroom including...)

Wish list for materials you need for your classroom:

Skills Checklist

If you are currently in the classroom, use the complete list on page 95 of this book as a frequent skills checklist to confirm that you are developing your teaching skills repertoire. You may either fill out the Skills Checklist yourself or ask a teacher to observe you and complete the Skills Checklist for you (peer evaluation). If you are unfamiliar with an item, read about it in the book or talk with your mentor or trainer. The following is an abbreviated checklist related to this module.

_____Teacher supports partnerships with parents through planning and implementing regular parent participation opportunities. (see page 24)

_____Teacher creates, maintains, and refreshes appropriate classroom environment. (see pages 67-69)

_____Classroom contains experiences and activities that reflect a wide variety of possibilities for children in the classroom. (see pages 24-29)

_____Teacher uses webbing as a technique to support emergent curriculum. (see page 25)

_____Classroom includes a wide variety of appropriate toys and materials. (see pages 24-29)

_____   _____

Teacher Completing Training Module   Date
(please sign and date)

Congratulations! You have completed Module 14 of 38 in the **Teacher's Guide**.

DRAMATIC POSSIBILITIES

Purpose: to understand what dramatic possibilities are and to create a teacher-made toy for the classroom from dramatic possibilities

TIME: APPROXIMATELY 1½ HOURS

Read about Dramatic Possibilities on page 25. Activities of this type are a favorite for both toddlers and teachers. Look around your classroom or another classroom in your school to see what dramatic possibilities materials are available. Make a list of what you find:

READ THIS

Now, look at one of the Possibilities Plans in the book. Find an activity that describes a dramatic possibilities toy that you would like to make for your classroom. Also, read page 233 for more information on making toys and finding materials.

READ THIS

What toy did you choose?

Gather the materials and create the teacher-made toy. Safety is a prime concern for teacher-made materials, so be sure to check the toy carefully for safety. Also ask your mentor or trainer to check the toy for safety before using it in your classroom.

_____   _____

Checked Toy for Safety   Date

Describe the toy that you made for your classroom.

How do you plan to use it?

Skills Checklist

If you are currently in the classroom, use the complete list on page 95 of this book as a frequent skills checklist to confirm that you are developing your teaching skills repertoire. You may either fill out the Skills Checklist yourself or ask a teacher to observe you and complete the Skills Checklist for you (peer evaluation). If you are unfamiliar with an item, read about it in the book or talk with your mentor or trainer. The following is an abbreviated checklist related to this module.

_____Teacher creates, maintains, and refreshes appropriate classroom environment. (see pages 67-69)

_____Classroom contains experiences and activities that reflect a wide variety of possibilities for children in the classroom. (see pages 24-29)

_____Teacher uses webbing as a technique to support emergent curriculum. (see page 25)

_____Classroom includes a wide variety of appropriate toys and materials. (see pages 24-29)

_____Classroom includes a variety of safe, appropriate, teacher-made toys. (see page 233)

_____   _____

Teacher Completing Training Module   Date
(please sign and date)

Congratulations! You have completed Module 15 of 38 in the **Teacher's Guide.**

SENSORY AND ART POSSIBILITIES

Purpose: to understand what sensory and art possibilities are and to create a teacher-made toy for the classroom from sensory and art possibilities

TIME: APPROXIMATELY 1 HOUR

Read about Sensory and Art Possibilities on pages 25-26. Look around your classroom or another classroom in your school to see what sensory and art possibilities materials are available. Make a list of what you find:

READ THIS

Now, look at one of the Possibilities Plans in the book. Find an activity that describes a sensory and art possibilities toy that you would like to make for your classroom. Also, read page 233 for more information on making toys and finding materials.

READ THIS

What toy did you choose?

Gather the materials and create the teacher-made toy. Safety is a prime concern for teacher-made materials, so be sure to check the toy carefully for safety. Also ask your mentor or trainer to check the toy for safety before using it in your classroom.

_____   _____

Checked Toy for Safety   Date

Describe the toy that you made for your classroom.

How do you plan to use it?

Skills Checklist

If you are currently in the classroom, use the complete list on page 95 of this book as a frequent skills checklist to confirm that you are developing your teaching skills repertoire. You may either fill out the Skills Checklist yourself or ask a teacher to observe you and complete the Skills Checklist for you (peer evaluation). If you are unfamiliar with an item, read about it in the book or talk with your mentor or trainer. The following is an abbreviated checklist related to this module.

_____Teacher creates, maintains, and refreshes appropriate classroom environment. (see pages 67-69)

_____Classroom contains experiences and activities that reflect a wide variety of possibilities for children in the classroom. (see pages 24-29)

_____Teacher uses webbing as a technique to support emergent curriculum. (see page 25)

_____Classroom includes a wide variety of appropriate toys and materials. (see pages 24-29)

_____Classroom includes a variety of safe, appropriate, teacher-made toys. (see page 233)

_____   _____

Teacher Completing Training Module   Date
(please sign and date)

Congratulations! You have completed Module 16 of 38 in the **Teacher's Guide.**

CURIOSITY POSSIBILITIES

Purpose: to understand what curiosity possibilities are and to create a teacher-made toy for the classroom from curiosity possibilities

TIME: APPROXIMATELY 1 HOUR

Read about Curiosity Possibilities on pages 26-27. Look around your classroom or another classroom in your school to see what curiosity possibilities materials are available. Make a list of what you find:

READ THIS

Now, look at one of the Possibilities Plans in the book. Find an activity that describes a curiosity possibilities toy that you would like to make for your classroom. Also, read page 233 for more information on making toys and finding materials.

READ THIS

What toy did you choose?

Gather the materials and create the teacher-made toy. Safety is a prime concern for teacher-made materials, so be sure to check the toy carefully for safety. Also ask your mentor or trainer to check the toy for safety before using it in your classroom.

_____   _____

Checked Toy for Safety   Date

Describe the toy that you made for your classroom.

How do you plan to use it?

Skills Checklist

If you are currently in the classroom, use the complete list on page 95 of this book as a frequent skills checklist to confirm that you are developing your teaching skills repertoire. You may either fill out the Skills Checklist yourself or ask a teacher to observe you and complete the Skills Checklist for you (peer evaluation). If you are unfamiliar with an item, read about it in the book or talk with your mentor or trainer. The following is an abbreviated checklist related to this module.

_____Teacher creates, maintains, and refreshes appropriate classroom environment. (see pages 67-69)

_____Classroom contains experiences and activities that reflect a wide variety of possibilities for children in the classroom. (see pages 24-29)

_____Teacher uses webbing as a technique to support emergent curriculum. (see page 25)

_____Classroom includes a wide variety of appropriate toys and materials. (see pages 24-29)

_____Classroom includes a variety of safe, appropriate, teacher-made toys. (see page 233)

_____   _____

Teacher Completing Training Module   Date
(please sign and date)

Congratulations! You have completed Module 17 of 38 in the **Teacher's Guide**.

CONSTRUCTION POSSIBILITIES

Purpose: to understand what construction possibilities are and to create a teacher-made toy for the classroom from construction possibilities

TIME: APPROXIMATELY 1 HOUR

Read about Construction Possibilities on page 27. Look around your classroom or another classroom in your school to see what construction possibilities materials are available. Make a list of what you find:

READ THIS

Now, look at one of the Possibilities Plans in the book. Find an activity that describes a construction possibilities toy that you would like to make for your classroom. Also, read page 233 for more information on making toys and finding materials.

READ THIS

What toy did you choose?

Gather the materials and create the teacher-made toy. Safety is a prime concern for teacher-made materials, so be sure to check the toy carefully for safety. Also ask your mentor or trainer to check the toy for safety before using it in your classroom.

_____   _____
Checked Toy for Safety   Date

Describe the toy that you made for your classroom.

How do you plan to use it?

Skills Checklist

If you are currently in the classroom, use the complete list on page 95 of this book as a frequent skills checklist to confirm that you are developing your teaching skills repertoire. You may either fill out the Skills Checklist yourself or ask a teacher to observe you and complete the Skills Checklist for you (peer evaluation). If you are unfamiliar with an item, read about it in the book or talk with your mentor or trainer. The following is an abbreviated checklist related to this module.

_____Teacher creates, maintains, and refreshes appropriate classroom environment. (see pages 67-69)

_____Classroom contains experiences and activities that reflect a wide variety of possibilities for children in the classroom. (see pages 24-29)

_____Teacher uses webbing as a technique to support emergent curriculum. (see page 25)

_____Classroom includes a wide variety of appropriate toys and materials. (see pages 24-29)

_____Classroom includes a variety of safe, appropriate, teacher-made toys. (see page 233)

_____   _____

Teacher Completing Training Module   Date
(please sign and date)

Congratulations! You have completed Module 18 of 38 in the **Teacher's Guide**.

LITERACY POSSIBILITIES

Purpose: to understand what literacy possibilities are and to create a teacher-made toy for the classroom from literacy possibilities

TIME: APPROXIMATELY I HOUR

Read about Literacy Possibilities on page 27. Look around your classroom or another classroom in your school to see what literacy possibilities materials are available. Make a list of what you find:

READ THIS

Now, look at one of the Possibilities Plans in the book. Find an activity that describes a literacy possibilities toy that you would like to make for your classroom. Also, read page 233 for more information on making toys and finding materials.

READ THIS

What toy did you choose?

Gather the materials and create the teacher-made toy. Safety is a prime concern for teacher-made materials, so be sure to check the toy carefully for safety. Also ask your mentor or trainer to check the toy for safety before using it in your classroom.

_____   _____

Checked Toy for Safety   Date

Describe the toy that you made for your classroom.

How do you plan to use it?

Skills Checklist

If you are currently in the classroom, use the complete list on page 95 of this book as a frequent skills checklist to confirm that you are developing your teaching skills repertoire. You may either fill out the Skills Checklist yourself or ask a teacher to observe you and complete the Skills Checklist for you (peer evaluation). If you are unfamiliar with an item, read about it in the book or talk with your mentor or trainer. The following is an abbreviated checklist related to this module.

_____Teacher creates, maintains, and refreshes appropriate classroom environment. (see pages 67-69)

_____Classroom contains experiences and activities that reflect a wide variety of possibilities for children in the classroom. (see pages 24-29)

_____Teacher uses webbing as a technique to support emergent curriculum. (see page 25)

_____Classroom includes a wide variety of appropriate toys and materials. (see pages 24-29)

_____Classroom includes a variety of safe, appropriate, teacher-made toys. (see page 233)

_____   _____

Teacher Completing Training Module   Date
(please sign and date)

Congratulations! You have completed Module 19 of 38 in the **Teacher's Guide**.

MUSIC AND MOVEMENT POSSIBILITIES

Purpose: to understand what music and movement possibilities are and to create a teacher-made toy for the classroom from music and movement possibilities

TIME: APPROXIMATELY 1 HOUR

READ THIS

Read about Music and Movement Possibilities on pages 28-29. Look around your classroom or another classroom in your school to see what music and movement possibilities materials are available. Make a list of what you find:

READ THIS

Now, look at one of the Possibilities Plans in the book. Find an activity that describes a movement possibilities toy that you would like to make for your classroom. Also, read page 233 for more information on making toys and finding materials.

What toy did you choose?

Gather the materials and create the teacher-made toy. Safety is a prime concern for teacher-made materials, so be sure to check the toy carefully for safety. Also ask your mentor or trainer to check the toy for safety before using it in your classroom.

_____   _____
Checked Toy for Safety   Date

Describe the toy that you made for your classroom.

How do you plan to use it?

Skills Checklist

If you are currently in the classroom, use the complete list on page 95 of this book as a frequent skills checklist to confirm that you are developing your teaching skills repertoire. You may either fill out the Skills Checklist yourself or ask a teacher to observe you and complete the Skills Checklist for you (peer evaluation). If you are unfamiliar with an item, read about it in the book or talk with your mentor or trainer. The following is an abbreviated checklist related to this module.

_____Teacher creates, maintains, and refreshes appropriate classroom environment. (see pages 67-69)

_____Classroom contains experiences and activities that reflect a wide variety of possibilities for children in the classroom. (see pages 24-29)

_____Teacher uses webbing as a technique to support emergent curriculum. (see page 25)

_____Classroom includes a wide variety of appropriate toys and materials. (see pages 24-29)

_____Classroom includes a variety of safe, appropriate, teacher-made toys. (see page 233)

_____   _____

Teacher Completing Training Module   Date
(please sign and date)

Congratulations! You have completed Module 20 of 38 in the **Teacher's Guide**.

OUTDOOR POSSIBILITIES

Purpose: to understand what outdoor possibilities are and to create a teacher-made toy for the classroom from outdoor possibilities

TIME: APPROXIMATELY 1 HOUR

Read about Outdoor Possibilities on page 29. Look around your classroom or another classroom in your school to see what outdoor possibilities materials are available. Make a list of what you find:

READ THIS

Now, look at one of the Possibilities Plans in the book. Find an activity that describes an outdoor possibilities toy that you would like to make. Also, read page 233 for more information on making toys and finding materials.

READ THIS

What toy did you choose?

Gather the materials and create the teacher-made toy. Safety is a prime concern for teacher-made materials, so be sure to check the toy carefully for safety. Also ask your mentor or trainer to check the toy for safety before using it in your classroom.

_____   _____

Checked Toy for Safety   Date

Describe the toy that you made for the outside.

How do you plan to use it?

Skills Checklist

If you are currently in the classroom, use the complete list on page 95 of this book as a frequent skills checklist to confirm that you are developing your teaching skills repertoire. You may either fill out the Skills Checklist yourself or ask a teacher to observe you and complete the Skills Checklist for you (peer evaluation). If you are unfamiliar with an item, read about it in the book or talk with your mentor or trainer. The following is an abbreviated checklist related to this module.

_____Teacher creates, maintains, and refreshes appropriate classroom environment. (see pages 67-69)
_____Classroom contains experiences and activities that reflect a wide variety of possibilities for children in the classroom. (see pages 24-29)
_____Teacher uses webbing as a technique to support emergent curriculum. (see page 25)
_____Classroom includes a wide variety of appropriate toys and materials. (see pages 24-29)
_____Classroom includes a variety of safe, appropriate, teacher-made toys. (see page 233)

_____   _____

Teacher Completing Training Module   Date
(please sign and date)

Congratulations! You have completed Module 21 of 38 in the **Teacher's Guide**.

PROJECT POSSIBILITIES

Purpose: to understand project possibilities and to plan one for the classroom

TIME: APPROXIMATELY 1 HOUR

Projects are repeated experiences that children have over time. (Activities that last one day or even a week probably are not projects.) By including projects in children's experiences, you can give children a sense of familiarity and security because activities are revisited. Read about projects in Getting Started on page 29. Then read about the project Bag Buildings for Parents on pages 181-182.

Each Possibilities Plan includes ideas for projects. Look on the planning pages or even in the table of contents to find the Project Possibilities.

Choose an activity from anywhere in the Possibilities Plan sections of the book and turn the activity into a project.

What activity did you choose? Write the title below with the page number.

How can you turn this activity into a project for toddlers?

Try the project with the toddlers in your classroom. Write what happened below.

Skills Checklist

If you are currently in the classroom, use the complete list on page 95 of this book as a frequent skills checklist to confirm that you are developing your teaching skills repertoire. You may either fill out the Skills Checklist yourself or ask a teacher to observe you and complete the Skills Checklist for you (peer evaluation). If you are unfamiliar with an item, read about it in the book or talk with your mentor or trainer. The following is an abbreviated checklist related to this module.

_____Classroom contains experiences and activities that reflect a wide variety of possibilities for children in the classroom. (see pages 24-29)

_____Teacher uses webbing as a technique to support emergent curriculum. (see page 25)

_____Classroom includes a wide variety of appropriate toys and materials. (see pages 24-29)

_____Classroom includes a variety of safe, appropriate, teacher-made toys. (see page 233)

_____Teacher uses projects to provide repeated experiences over time for toddlers. (see page 29)

_____   _____

Teacher Completing Training Module   Date
(please sign and date)

Congratulations! You have completed Module 22 of 38 in the **Teacher's Guide**.

PARENT PARTICIPATION POSSIBILITIES

Purpose: to learn about, plan, and implement parent participation activities that will help support parent partnerships

TIME: APPROXIMATELY 1 HOUR

Parents are so important in the lives of their children, and teachers are in a position to support them by creating partnerships with parents. *Innovations: The Comprehensive Toddler Curriculum* has numerous ideas to help you in that role.

Each chapter contains a section called Innovations in Parent Partnerships, which includes suggestions for school-initiated possibilities (such as collecting materials to be made into toys for the classroom), parent participation activities (such as invitations for parents to come to a parent meeting), parent postcards to give to parents (which include topics to assist parents in understanding and supporting their child's growth and development), and additional resources for parents (pages 58-67, 142-157, 227-230, 308-319, 391-402, 474-484). In addition to all these options, you also can find ideas on how to get parents involved in activities and additional postcards in all the different Possibilities Plans. For example, in Possibilities Plan: Me and My Body, see the Parent Participation Possibilities section on pages 87-89 for participation ideas and postcards.

READ THIS

To support partnerships with parents, plan activities for parents for the next two weeks. What ideas have you chosen? Write them below.

How will you communicate with parents about these activities?

How will you prepare for the events?

How did the planned event go?

What will you do differently next time?

Skills Checklist

If you are currently in the classroom, use the complete list on page 95 of this book as a frequent skills checklist to confirm that you are developing your teaching skills repertoire. You may either fill out the Skills Checklist yourself or ask a teacher to observe you and complete the Skills Checklist for you (peer evaluation). If you are unfamiliar with an item, read about it in the book or talk with your mentor or trainer. The following is an abbreviated checklist related to this module.

_____Classroom contains experiences and activities that reflect a wide variety of possibilities for children in the classroom. (see pages 24-29)

_____Teacher uses webbing as a technique to support emergent curriculum. (see page 25)

_____Classroom includes a wide variety of appropriate toys and materials. (see pages 24-29)

_____Classroom includes a variety of safe, appropriate, teacher-made toys. (see page 233)

_____Teacher uses projects to provide repeated experiences over time for toddlers. (see page 29)

_____Teacher plans, implements, and evaluates the success of parent participation activities.

_____   _____

Teacher Completing Training Module   Date
(please sign and date)

Congratulations! You have completed Module 23 of 38 in the **Teacher's Guide**.

CONCEPTS LEARNED

Purpose: to explain how to use Concepts Learned in the Classroom and how to use these lists as one way to communicate to parents about their child's experiences in the classroom

TIME: APPROXIMATELY 1 HOUR

It is often difficult for parents to see the important interactive experiences that toddlers are having in school as learning activities. ***Innovations: The Comprehensive Toddler Curriculum*** has a strategy for helping you share with parents what children are learning. Concepts Learned lists are provided for each Possibilities Plan, and you can use these lists in a variety of ways.

The easiest way to use the Concepts Learned list is to copy the appropriate list from the appendix and post it in the classroom. When posted, parents will be able to see the content and process learning that is taking place in your classroom.

To make the list come alive for individual children and their parents, use the list to document children's learning. For example, using the Concepts Learned list from the Me and My Body Possibilities Plan (page 90), you might put the child's name and date next to the concept learned by each child.

Example:

I can recognize myself in a mirror. Julia, 10/5
I can play interactive games. Mike, 10/26
I can play near another child.
I can point to named body parts (eyes, ears, nose, mouth, chin, elbow, arm, knee, ankle, wrist, and so on). Kaylee knows eyes, ears, and nose. 10/11
Bret knows "chinny chin chin." 10/1
Sophie knows eyes and nose. 10/15
I can name body parts. Kathy, 11/1
Eyes are for seeing.
Noses are for smelling. Mary, 9/30
Mouths are for eating.
Ears are for hearing.
I can play chase.
I can climb two- or three-step stairs. Jean, 10/2
I can roll a ball.
I can turn the pages of a book.
I can ride a small riding toy without pedals.
I can jump in place.
I can hop on one foot.
I can walk with balance. Chris, 10/31
I can walk on tiptoes.

I can match pictures.
I can eat with a spoon. *Louisa, 10/21*
I can name pictured items. *Sun Li, 10/18*
I can use glue sticks and art materials to create a project.
I can follow one-step and two-step directions.
I can take things off.
I can put things on. *Rosanna, 10/6*

You might choose to edit the list from the book, adding additional concepts learned from other experiences provided by you. You may also find it helpful to number the concepts on a Concepts Learned list and then use these numbers when completing anecdotal observations.

Concepts Learned are important for parents because they let them know what you and their child have been doing and what the results are. Concepts are very simple—relating to things that toddlers can understand. Both content and process knowledge are included. For example, using the Concepts Learned list for Me and My Body (page 90), one example of content knowledge is "Noses are for smelling," and one example of process knowledge is "I can take things off."

Select a Concepts Learned list from the appendix. Observe a classroom for about 15-20 minutes, using the list to assess what children are learning. Add additional items to the list that become apparent during your observation. Discuss your observation with your mentor or trainer.

List the items that you added to Concepts Learned.

Observation discussed with _____.
                              (Name)   (Date)

Skills Checklist

If you are currently in the classroom, use the complete list on page 95 of this book as a frequent skills checklist to confirm that you are developing your teaching skills repertoire. You may either fill out the Skills Checklist yourself or ask a teacher to observe you and complete the Skills Checklist for you (peer evaluation). If you are unfamiliar with an item, read about it in the book or talk with your mentor or trainer. The following is an abbreviated checklist related to this module.

_____Classroom includes a wide variety of appropriate toys and materials. (see pages 24-29)

_____Classroom includes a variety of safe, appropriate, teacher-made toys. (see page 233)

_____Teacher uses projects to provide repeated experiences over time for toddlers. (see page 29)

_____Teacher plans, implements, and evaluates the success of parent participation activities.

_____Teacher uses Concepts Learned to communicate with parents about their children. (see pages 30-31, 558-569)

_____   _____

Teacher Completing Training Module   Date
(please sign and date)

Congratulations! You have completed Module 24 of 38 in the **Teacher's Guide**.

MODULE 25 RESOURCES

Purpose: to explore the resources sections of the book to support learning for toddlers

TIME: APPROXIMATELY I HOUR

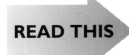

Read about the resources available to you to support learning for toddlers (page 31). Then look through one of the resources sections in the book found in each Possibilities Plan (pages 90-92 in Me and My Body; pages 116-120 in My Family; pages 185-189 in My Neighborhood; pages 211-213 in Fruits and Vegetables; pages 258-260 in Space; pages 277-279 in Sky; pages 343-346 in Big Animals; pages 364-366 in Little Animals; pages 425-428 in Construction; pages 449-452 in Wheels; pages 504-506 in Storybook Characters; pages 529-533 in Water).

After reading one of the resources sections, practice filling out a Possibilities Plan. Use the partial section of a blank Possibilities Plan below and write in the appropriate sections what you have chosen from the resources section. See pages 556-557 for an example.

Dramatic Possibilities

Art/Sensory Possibilities

Curiosity Possibilities

Construction Possibilities

Music/Movement Possibilities

Literacy Possibilities

Outdoor Possibilities

Project Possibilities

Books	Picture File Pictures/Vocabulary

Rhymes & Fingerplays	Music/Songs	Prop Boxes

Skills Checklist

If you are currently in the classroom, use the complete list on page 95 of this book as a frequent skills checklist to confirm that you are developing your teaching skills repertoire. You may either fill out the Skills Checklist yourself or ask a teacher to observe you and complete the Skills Checklist for you (peer evaluation). If you are unfamiliar with an item, read about it in the book or talk with your mentor or trainer. The following is an abbreviated checklist related to this module.

_____Classroom includes a wide variety of appropriate toys and materials. (see pages 24-29)

_____Classroom includes a variety of safe, appropriate, teacher-made toys. (see page 233)

_____Teacher uses projects to provide repeated experiences over time for toddlers. (see page 29)

_____Teacher plans, implements, and evaluates the success of parent participation activities.

_____Teacher uses Concepts Learned to communicate with parents about their children. (see pages 30-31, 558-569)

_____Teacher identifies resources needed as a part of the planning process.

_____   _____

Teacher Completing Training Module   Date
(please sign and date)

Congratulations! You have completed Module 25 of 38 in the **Teacher's Guide**.

PROP BOXES

Purpose: to learn about prop boxes and make one to use with toddlers in the classroom

TIME: APPROXIMATELY 1 HOUR

Prop boxes are a way to organize materials that support particular topics in the classroom. Many teachers use copy paper boxes or clear plastic tubs with tops. Label the box (for example, things that go on my head, parents at work, cleaning up, or construction) and plan a place to store prop boxes while they are not in use.

Gather materials to place in the prop box. Check them for safety and ask your mentor or trainer to check the items for safety as well. Plan how to use the prop box in your classroom.

_____   _____

Checked Prop Box Items for Safety   Date

What did you write on the label of the prop box you made?

What materials did you include in the prop box?

How do you plan to use the prop box in the classroom?

Where will you store the prop box when not in use?

Skills Checklist

If you are currently in the classroom, use the complete list on page 95 of this book as a frequent skills checklist to confirm that you are developing your teaching skills repertoire. You may either fill out the Skills Checklist yourself or ask a teacher to observe you and complete the Skills Checklist for you (peer evaluation). If you are unfamiliar with an item, read about it in the book or talk with your mentor or trainer. The following is an abbreviated checklist related to this module.

_____Teacher uses projects to provide repeated experiences over time for toddlers. (see page 29)

_____Teacher plans, implements, and evaluates the success of parent participation activities.

_____Teacher uses Concepts Learned to communicate with parents about their children. (see pages 30-31, 558-569)

_____Teacher identifies resources needed as part of the planning process.

_____Teacher uses prop boxes to gather, organize, and store appropriate materials for use on particular topics in the classroom. (see page 553)

_____   _____

Teacher Completing Training Module   Date
(please sign and date)

Congratulations! You have completed Module 26 of 38 in the *Teacher's Guide*.

PICTURE FILE/VOCABULARY

Purpose: to learn about picture files and vocabulary lists and to begin using both in the classroom

TIME: APPROXIMATELY 1 HOUR

Read the information about picture files/vocabulary on page 31. Also, read some of the lists given for picture files/vocabulary in the Possibilities sections.

Toddlers are building cognitive images of the things they are experiencing. Pictures help give children a variety of different images, and they also add information to the images that the toddlers have already experienced.

Begin a picture file by cutting out pictures from magazines, calendars, and posters. Look for pictures that show one image clearly. Trim the edges, attach them to construction paper or cardboard, and laminate or cover them with clear contact paper. Use file folders to sort the pictures by category (for example, families, babies, feet/shoes, hands, faces, furniture, cars, trucks, houses, and so on). Use the pictures to provide cognitive images.

You can add pictures to the environment at children's eye level, attached to the floor to provide images as children scoot or crawl about the environment, or put them together to form simple children's books. Picture files are a source of novelty in the classroom because you can change the photographs from the file to match the topics of Possibilities Plans, to reflect the interests of the children, or to highlight interesting happenings in the larger social world of the child or school.

Picture file pictures also provide acceptance and validation of the diverse images of people who are in our world. Use them to connect children to images from their own culture and ethnic group as well as to diversify the images children have of others. You can also use photographs and pictures as support for emerging literacy skills by pointing out and naming images in the pictures.

You can support toddlers' vocabulary development as you interact with them throughout the day. Focus on adding words that are new and related to the Possibilities Plans. Write these words in lower case letters with photos, pictures, or illustrations of the word on the page.

Try to use the words frequently in verbal interactions, and in fingerplays and songs with toddlers.

What picture file/vocabulary categories have you started? List them below. Under each category, list the individual pictures you have collected.

Category _____

    _____

    _____

    _____

    _____

Category _____

    _____

    _____

    _____

    _____

Category _____

    _____

    _____

    _____

    _____

Skills Checklist

If you are currently in the classroom, use the complete list on page 95 of this book as a frequent skills checklist to confirm that you are developing your teaching skills repertoire. You may either fill out the Skills Checklist yourself or ask a teacher to observe you and complete the Skills Checklist for you (peer evaluation). If you are unfamiliar with an item, read about it in the book or talk with your mentor or trainer. The following is an abbreviated checklist related to this module.

_____Teacher uses projects to provide repeated experiences over time for toddlers. (see page 29)

_____Teacher plans, implements, and evaluates the success of parent participation activities.

_____Teacher uses Concepts Learned to communicate with parents about their children. (see pages 30-31, 558-569)

_____Teacher uses prop boxes to gather, organize, and store appropriate materials for use on particular topics in the classroom. (see page 553)

_____Teacher uses picture files and vocabulary to support children's learning about diversity and emerging literacy skills. (see page 31)

_____   _____

Teacher Completing Training Module   Date
(please sign and date)

Congratulations! You have completed Module 27 of 38 in the **Teacher's Guide**.

BOOKS

Purpose: to explore the importance of books in the classroom, to read to each toddler every day, and to create a Books Read List

TIME: APPROXIMATELY 1 HOUR

Reading is a natural part of the early childhood classroom. Through early, positive exposure to reading, children start down the road of literacy development. It is important to read books to each child every day. Keeping a Books Read List communicates to parents what you and the toddlers are doing during the day and is a part of the documentation of learning in the classroom. Imagine a parent's excitement at seeing the Books Read List beginning to grow and grow, validating that you are spending important one-on-one time with their toddler and that you are stimulating the child's emerging interest in the written word.

A form for the Books Read List is in this book on page 109. Each Possibilities section includes suggested books, and often activities in the literacy possibilities are book-related. If you are already in the classroom, begin your own Books Read List and post it in the classroom. Later, you will want to copy the list for each child's portfolio or begin an individual list as the child's interest in particular books emerges. Don't hesitate to put a book on the list more than once! Repetition forms the foundation of interest in more than the pictures—in the words, the direction of reading (left to right), and the story that the words tell on each page.

Where are children's books located in your school?

What is your favorite book for toddlers?

How do you plan to use it in the classroom?

List some additional ways to get books into your classroom.

Skills Checklist

If you are currently in the classroom, use the complete list on page 95 of this book as a frequent skills checklist to confirm that you are developing your teaching skills repertoire. You may either fill out the Skills Checklist yourself or ask a teacher to observe you and complete the Skills Checklist for you (peer evaluation). If you are unfamiliar with an item, read about it in the book or talk with your mentor or trainer. The following is an abbreviated checklist related to this module.

_____Teacher uses projects to provide repeated experiences over time for toddlers. (see page 29)

_____Teacher plans, implements, and evaluates the success of parent participation activities.

_____Teacher uses Concepts Learned to communicate with parents about their children. (see pages 30-31, 558-569)

_____Teacher uses prop boxes to gather, organize, and store appropriate materials for use on particular topics in the classroom. (see page 553)

_____Teacher uses picture files and vocabulary to support children's learning about diversity and emerging literacy skills. (see page 31)

_____Teacher reads to each child every day. (see pages 320-321)

_____   _____
Teacher Completing Training Module   Date
(please sign and date)

Congratulations! You have completed Module 28 of 38 in the **Teacher's Guide**.

RHYMES/FINGERPLAYS

Purpose: to explore the use of rhymes and fingerplays in the toddler classroom, to learn a new rhyme, and to use a new rhyme in the classroom

TIME: APPROXIMATELY 1 HOUR

Rhymes and fingerplays are wonderful ways to support early literacy development for toddlers. Use them throughout the day as you interact with toddlers. Read through the section of songs, poems, rhymes, and fingerplays in the appendix (pages 570-579), and choose a new rhyme or fingerplay to learn and use with toddlers.

READ THIS

Which rhyme/fingerplay did you choose?

How did you use it in the classroom?

What was the child's (children's) reaction during the first exposure?

Will you use the rhyme/fingerplay in a different way the next time you use it? How?

What is the child's (children's) reaction after you have used the fingerplay many times?

Skills Checklist

If you are currently in the classroom, use the complete list on page 95 of this book as a frequent skills checklist to confirm that you are developing your teaching skills repertoire. You may either fill out the Skills Checklist yourself or ask a teacher to observe you and complete the Skills Checklist for you (peer evaluation). If you are unfamiliar with an item, read about it in the book or talk with your mentor or trainer. The following is an abbreviated checklist related to this module.

_____Teacher plans, implements, and evaluates the success of parent participation activities.

_____Teacher uses Concepts Learned to communicate with parents about their children. (see pages 30-31, 558-569)

_____Teacher uses prop boxes to gather, organize, and store appropriate materials for use on particular topics in the classroom. (see page 553)

_____Teacher uses picture files and vocabulary to support children's learning about diversity and emerging literacy skills. (see page 31)

_____Teacher reads to each child every day. (see pages 320-321)

_____Teacher uses rhymes/fingerplays while interacting with toddlers throughout the day. (pages 570-579)

_____   _____

Teacher Completing Training Module   Date
(please sign and date)

Congratulations! You have completed Module 29 of 38 in the **Teacher's Guide**.

MUSIC/SONGS

Purpose: to explore the use of music/songs in the toddler classroom, to learn a new song, and to use a new song in the classroom

TIME: APPROXIMATELY 1 HOUR

Music and songs are wonderful ways to support early literacy development for toddlers. Use them throughout the day as you interact with toddlers and as you transition from one activity to another. Some research suggests a close link between music experiences and later math abilities. Include music and songs as a natural part of every day. Read through the section on songs, poems, rhymes, and fingerplays in the Appendix (pages 570-579). Choose a new song to learn and use with toddlers.

READ THIS

Which song did you choose?

How did you use it in the classroom?

What was the child's (children's) reaction to the song?

Will you use the song in a different way next time? How?

Skills Checklist

If you are currently in the classroom, use the complete list on page 95 of this book as a frequent skills checklist to confirm that you are developing your teaching skills repertoire. You may either fill out the Skills Checklist yourself or ask a teacher to observe you and complete the Skills Checklist for you (peer evaluation). If you are unfamiliar with an item, read about it in the book or talk with your mentor or trainer. The following is an abbreviated checklist related to this module.

_____Teacher uses prop boxes to gather, organize, and store appropriate materials for use on particular topics in the classroom. (see page 553)

_____Teacher uses picture files and vocabulary to support children's learning about diversity and emerging literacy skills. (see page 31)

_____Teacher reads to each child every day. (see pages 320-321)

_____Teacher uses rhymes/fingerplays while interacting with toddlers throughout the day. (see pages 570-579)

_____Teacher uses music/songs during the day for interaction and to assist with transitions. (see pages 570-579)

_____   _____

Teacher Completing Training Module   Date
(please sign and date)

Congratulations! You have completed Module 30 of 38 in the **Teacher's Guide**.

TOYS AND MATERIALS (GATHERED AND BOUGHT)

Purpose: to create a storage and sanitation system for toys and materials in the classroom

TIME: APPROXIMATELY 1 HOUR

Read the section "Welcoming Environments for Toddlers" on pages 157-160 under Innovations in Environments. Toys and materials are important elements in the toddler classroom. Each Possibilities section contains many suggestions for the use of toys and materials, as well as a cumulative list of both gathered and bought materials, to support the activities and experiences contained in the section.

READ THIS

Provide duplicate items since toddlers do not share. Store toys and materials on low, sturdy shelves in clear, open containers. Because toddlers still explore items by mouthing them, you need to have a system for storing and sanitizing toys and materials.

Disinfect items that toddlers put into their mouths by washing them with soap and water, and then rinsing them in a bleach-and-water solution of ¼ cup bleach to 1 gallon of water. Allow them to air dry. Proper mixing of the bleach water solution is important. Too little bleach will not accomplish the disinfecting; too much bleach is hard on toy surfaces and hands. Keep a measuring cup nearby to make sure you mix the solution correctly. You can also sanitize some toys and materials in a dishwasher. When using an appliance, follow the manufacturer's instructions for adequate sanitation.

Regular sanitation after each use decreases the sharing of colds and other contagious conditions caused by germs contaminating surfaces. Many teachers prefer to use a shallow tub in which to place contaminated items until they can be disinfected. (Keep the tub out of the reach of children.) Clearly label containers that have contaminated toys in them to prevent reintroducing them into the classroom before they are sanitized. Always keep bleach in a locked cabinet away from children and bleach solutions out of the reach of children. While disinfecting toys and materials, inspect them for safety. Repair or discard unsafe items immediately.

Find out what the system for the storage and sanitation of toys and materials is at your school, or create a system in your classroom. Describe your system below.

Skills Checklist

If you are currently in the classroom, use the complete list on page 95 of this book as a frequent skills checklist to confirm that you are developing your teaching skills repertoire. You may either fill out the Skills Checklist yourself or ask a teacher to observe you and complete the Skills Checklist for you (peer evaluation). If you are unfamiliar with an item, read about it in the book or talk with your mentor or trainer. The following is an abbreviated checklist related to this module.

_____Teacher uses picture files and vocabulary to support children's learning about diversity and emerging literacy skills. (see page 31)

_____Teacher reads to each child every day. (see pages 320-321)

_____Teacher uses rhymes/fingerplays while interacting with toddlers throughout the day. (see pages 570-579)

_____Teacher uses music/songs during the day for interaction and to assist with transitions. (see pages 570-579)

_____Teacher uses a system for storing and disinfecting toys and materials. (see pages 157-160)

_____   _____

Teacher Completing Training Module   Date
(please sign and date)

Congratulations! You have completed Module 31 of 38 in the **Teacher's Guide**.

USING ANECDOTAL OBSERVATIONS

Purpose: to complete anecdotal observations

TIME: APPROXIMATELY 1 HOUR

Read about anecdotal notes on page 228, "Seeing Children as Unique" on page 19, and "Using Observation and Assessment Strategies" on page 21 in *Innovations: The Comprehensive Toddler Curriculum*.

Anecdotal observations of children at play are the foundation of understanding each child's individual developmental pace, unique temperamental traits, and stage of development. Anecdotal observations also serve as a way to uncover play themes and children's emerging interests. You can learn a lot from observing. For example, you might learn when toys and materials lose interest to children or when children need a little less challenge from the environment, toys and materials, and experiences. Additionally, anecdotal observations serve as a record of what is occurring in the classroom (documentation). Finally, observations form the foundation of information to be exchanged with parents during conferences.

Observation is an active process. Good teachers are always observing, and good teachers are always recording their observations to use later as springboards for reflection. *Innovations: The Comprehensive Toddler Curriculum* suggests that you observe children regularly and record your observations using Anecdotal Records.

An Anecdotal Record is a specific type of written record of an observation. When making an Anecdotal Record, record only objective information in your observation notes. Focus on what you see, when you see it, how it happens, where the child is, and what is happening. All of these notes are objective. Do not record what you *think* about what you see; just record what is happening.

Then take your observational notes and review them. Look for insight into a child's individual age or stage, ideas about interests and abilities, trends in play, indications that a skill is developing or has developed, and for curriculum ideas that might interest the child.

The following is an example of an anecdotal observation.

Anecdotal Record

Child Ashley Hill   **Date** July 23, 2001   **Time** 9:40

What I observed Ashley dumped out the plastic containers of small blocks and placed them one by one into a shopping cart. Then she pushed the cart to the toddler kitchen and placed the blocks into three pots on the stove. Other children observed but did not interfere. Later Ashley said, "Eat up!".

Teacher Miss Tasha

Anecdotal Record

Child   **Date**   **Time**

What I observed

Teacher

Observe three different children. Make three copies of the blank Anecdotal Record and complete one form for each child. Then complete the following tasks for each Anecdotal Record.

Identify the interest the child is showing or demonstrating that you might build a Possibilities Plan around.

Identify which subtask the child is demonstrating or working on.

Identify an emerging developmental domain (such as physical, language, cognitive, and so on) that the child is learning that could be enhanced by a teacher-made toy or a special-directed activity.

Skills Checklist

If you are currently in the classroom, use the complete list on page 95 of this book as a frequent skills checklist to confirm that you are developing your teaching skills repertoire. You may either fill out the Skills Checklist yourself or ask a teacher to observe you and complete the Skills Checklist for you (peer evaluation). If you are unfamiliar with an item, read about it in the book or talk with your mentor or trainer. The following is an abbreviated checklist related to this module.

_____Teacher reads to each child every day. (see pages 320-321)

_____Teacher uses picture files and vocabulary to support children's learning about diversity and emerging literacy skills. (see page 31)

_____Teacher uses music/songs during the day for interaction and to assist with transitions. (see pages 570-579)

_____Teacher uses a system for storing and disinfecting toys and materials. (see pages 157-160)

_____Teacher uses anecdotal observations to document learning in the classroom. (see pages 19, 21, 228)

_____   _____

Teacher Completing Training Module   Date
(please sign and date)

Congratulations! You have completed Module 32 of 38 in the **Teacher's Guide**.

PUTTING IT ALL TOGETHER TO PLAN FOR TEACHING

Purpose: to plan for teaching through completing a Possibilities Plan

TIME: APPROXIMATELY 2 HOURS

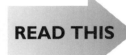
READ THIS

Read about possibilities planning on pages 551-557. After exploring all the individual elements found in *Innovations: The Comprehensive Toddler Curriculum*, you are now prepared to complete an entire Possibilities Plan for your classroom. Choose one of the possibilities sections and begin by reading the web. Use the web as it appears in the book, use a variation of it, or create your own web from scratch. The web will allow you to be flexible in your direction with activities and experiences in the classroom and reflect the children's unique interests and skills.

Copy the blank Possibilities Plan on pages 554-555 or use the one provided on pages 106-107 of this book. Copy your web in the space provided. Use the directions on pages 551-553 and fill in all the sections. Use the sample on pages 556-557 for assistance.

Post the Possibilities Plan in a convenient place in the classroom, so you can refer to it during the day. Parents will enjoy seeing your plan for learning. After you have finished the Possibilities Plan for the toddlers in your classroom, file it for reference as you develop other plans.

Skills Checklist

If you are currently in the classroom, use the complete list on page 95 of this book as a frequent skills checklist to confirm that you are developing your teaching skills repertoire. You may either fill out the Skills Checklist yourself or ask a teacher to observe you and complete the Skills Checklist for you (peer evaluation). If you are unfamiliar with an item, read about it in the book or talk with your mentor or trainer. The following is an abbreviated checklist related to this module.

_____Teacher reads to each child every day. (see pages 320-321)

_____Teacher uses picture files and vocabulary to support children's learning about diversity and emerging literacy skills. (see page 31)

_____Teacher uses music/songs during the day for interaction and to assist with transitions. (see pages 570-579)

_____Teacher uses a system for storing and disinfecting toys and materials. (see pages 157-160)

_____Teacher uses anecdotal observations to document learning in the classroom. (see pages 19, 21, 228)

_____Teacher has complete and appropriate Possibilities Plan posted in the classroom and uses it to provide activities and experiences for toddlers. (see pages 551-557)

_____   _____

Teacher Completing Training Module   Date
(please sign and date)

Congratulations! You have completed Module 33 of 38 in the **Teacher's Guide**.

MODULE 34

HOW TO USE FORMS TO DOCUMENT CHILDREN'S LEARNING, EVENTS, AND INTERACTIONS

Purpose: to practice using forms to document events, progress, and interactions in the classroom

TIME: APPROXIMATELY 1 HOUR

Documentation of events, progress, and interactions in the classroom is an important part of a teacher's job. Through your experiences thus far in the toddler classroom and/or your activities completed as a part of your training, you have already used a number of the forms contained in *Innovations: The Comprehensive Toddler Curriculum*. This training module will give you an opportunity to complete any of the forms you have not yet used. Fill in any of the following blank forms that you have not yet used. Fill in any of the following blank forms. If you need assistance, refer to the pages listed or talk with your mentor or trainer.

Observation/Assessment Instrument (see pages 18-22, 542-547)
Anecdotal Records (see pages 21, 228, 536)
Books Read List (see pages 320-321, 538)
Communication Sheet (see pages 471-472, 537)
Parent Visit Log (see pages 142, 541)
Accident/Incident Form (see pages 389, 447-448, 539-540)

Skills Checklist

If you are currently in the classroom, use the complete list on page 95 of this book as a frequent skills checklist to confirm that you are developing your teaching skills repertoire. You may either fill out the Skills Checklist yourself or ask a teacher to observe you and complete the Skills Checklist for you (peer evaluation). If you are unfamiliar with an item, read about it in the book or talk with your mentor or trainer. The following is an abbreviated checklist related to this module.

_____Teacher uses picture files and vocabulary to support children's learning about diversity and emerging literacy skills. (see page 31)

_____Teacher uses music/songs during the day for interaction and to assist with transitions. (see pages 570-579)

_____Teacher uses a system for storing and disinfecting toys and materials. (see pages 157-160)

_____Teacher uses anecdotal observations to document learning in the classroom. (see pages 19, 21, 228)

_____Teacher has complete and appropriate Possibilities Plan posted in the classroom and uses it to provide activities and experiences for toddlers. (see pages 551-557)

_____Teacher completes forms to document events, progress, and interactions in the classroom. (see pages 18-22, 142, 228, 389, 447-448, 471-472, 536-557)

_____   _____

Teacher Completing Training Module   Date
(please sign and date)

Congratulations! You have completed Module 34 of 38 in the **_Teacher's Guide_**.

CONFERENCING WITH PARENTS

Purpose: to learn about conferencing with parents and to have a simulated conference with parents using a variety of materials

TIME: APPROXIMATELY I HOUR

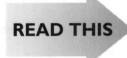

Read an explanation of conferencing (pages 467-472). Using the completed developmental assessment on pages 114-121, plan a conference and answer the following questions. Then, simulate conducting an actual conference with parents. Ask your coworkers or your mentor or trainer to role play the part of the parents.

How can you use the assessment to plan a conference with parents?

Write a sentence to show how you can welcome the parent and put him or her at ease.

Write three open-ended questions you can ask based on the results of the assessment.

How can you conclude the conference and make the parent feel comfortable asking questions?

How will you also use anecdotal notes, communication sheets, portfolios, and the Books Read List to make the conference informative and helpful for parents?

Skills Checklist

If you are currently in the classroom, use the complete list on page 95 of this book as a frequent skills checklist to confirm that you are developing your teaching skills repertoire. You may either fill out the Skills Checklist yourself or ask a teacher to observe you and complete the Skills Checklist for you (peer evaluation). If you are unfamiliar with an item, read about it in the book or talk with your mentor or trainer. The following is an abbreviated checklist related to this module.

_____Teacher uses music/songs during the day for interaction and to assist with transitions. (see pages 570-579)

_____Teacher uses a system for storing and disinfecting toys and materials. (see pages 157-160)

_____Teacher uses anecdotal observations to document learning in the classroom. (see pages 19, 21, 228)

_____Teacher has complete and appropriate Possibilities Plan posted in the classroom and uses it to provide activities and experiences for toddlers. (see pages 551-557)

_____Teacher completes forms to document events, progress, and interactions in the classroom. (see pages 18-22, 142, 228, 389, 447-448, 471-472, 536-557)

_____Teacher has periodic conferences with parents using a variety of materials. (see pages 467-472)

_____   _____

Teacher Completing Training Module   Date
(please sign and date)

Congratulations! You have completed Module 35 of 38 in the **Teacher's Guide**.

HOW TO USE PARENT POSTCARDS TO SUPPORT FAMILIES

Purpose: to plan for and use Parent Postcards to support families

TIME: APPROXIMATELY 1 HOUR

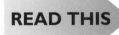
READ THIS

Parent Postcards are an important way to educate parents, establish teachers as the experts in the classroom, and keep parents involved in the education of their children. Read the explanation of postcards as well as the dissemination schedule in the appendix (pages 548-550).

Give out Parent Postcards in chronological order, by topic, or as needs and interests arise. You may give out Parent Postcards more than once. Repetition allows parents to reconsider information or to access it when they "need" to know about the topic.

This section of the curriculum is designed to grow. As you read the professional literature, newspapers, or magazines, look for interesting articles that might appeal to parents. Make copies of these to add to the Parent Postcards. When you find an article of interest, identify when it might be useful to parents and add the title to the dissemination schedule on pages 548-550. That way you will remember to use it again in the future.

You also may choose to write some of your own postcards. For example, you might write a postcard that introduces you to new parents, one that describes your philosophy of early education, or even one that tells parents more about the types of experience you have had in early education. Or, if you have a particular expertise, such as sensory experiences or outdoor play, write a postcard to share your special knowledge.

Plan how you will use Parent Postcards for children during the next four weeks. If you are already in the classroom, list the toddlers in your classroom and plan which postcards will be given out to the parents of each individual child.

Children's Names	Postcards
Michael	Creating a Separation and Reunion Ritual, page 60

Skills Checklist

If you are currently in the classroom, use the complete list on page 95 of this book as a frequent skills checklist to confirm that you are developing your teaching skills repertoire. You may either fill out the Skills Checklist yourself or ask a teacher to observe you and complete the Skills Checklist for you (peer evaluation). If you are unfamiliar with an item, read about it in the book or talk with your mentor or trainer. The following is an abbreviated checklist related to this module.

_____Teacher uses anecdotal observations to document learning in the classroom. (see pages 19, 21, 228)

_____Teacher has complete and appropriate Possibilities Plan posted in the classroom and uses it to provide activities and experiences for toddlers. (see pages 551-557)

_____Teacher completes forms to document events, progress, and interactions in the classroom. (see pages 18-22, 142, 228, 389, 447-448, 471-472, 536-557)

_____Teacher has periodic conferences with parents using a variety of materials. (see pages 467-472)

_____Teacher plans for and uses Parent Postcards and other resources to support families. (see pages 548-550)

_____   _____

Teacher Completing Training Module   Date
(please sign and date)

Congratulations! You have completed Module 36 of 38 in the **Teacher's Guide**.

HOW CAN I CONTINUE PROFESSIONAL DEVELOPMENT?

Purpose: to explore ways to continue professional development and to begin a specific plan

TIME: APPROXIMATELY 1 HOUR

The need to grow and learn is a requirement for all individuals, not just children. As an early childhood professional, you will want to continue your professional development so you will continue to grow as a teacher and improve your teaching skills.

The teaching competencies, contained under the Innovations in Teaching section in each chapter, are a great place to start. Start by rating yourself on each item as a self-evaluation. You may also want to ask a colleague or peer to use the list to evaluate your performance in the classroom and recommend areas for further development. Also, use the complete Skills Checklist in this book (pages 95-96) as an evaluation of your emerging skills. Particularly look to see how many of the skills you feel are already in place.

Another source of professional development is to read publications of professional associations. National Association for the Education of Young Children (NAEYC) is the professional association of early childhood educators. It publishes a journal, holds an annual conference, and provides a variety of membership services. Find out if your community has a local or state affiliate of NAEYC and join the association. NAEYC has both a web site (www.naeyc.org) and a toll-free number (800-424-2460).

One of your professional responsibilities is to document all of the formal and informal training in which you participate. Your school may want a record as well to meet licensing or accreditation requirements. You should maintain a current list of all training opportunities in which you participate. Keep copies of brochures announcing the training, training attendance certificates, or registration confirmation as a regular part of your training documentation.

It is also helpful to identify how you will apply the knowledge or information you gain through training opportunities. Reflecting on what you learned and how you will apply it deepens the value of almost any training experience and is part of professional reflective practice.

If you have not already done so, make a plan to pursue further formal training. Begin work towards your CDA or begin course work for an undergraduate or graduate degree. Formal professional development is strongly associated with positive outcomes for children in early childhood programs, so pursuing further professional training is a great way to advance your professional skills while guaranteeing positive outcomes for toddlers.

Write a paragraph below on how you plan to continue your professional development. Provide specific dates, phone numbers, and goals.

Skills Checklist

If you are currently in the classroom, use the complete list on page 95 of this book as a frequent skills checklist to confirm that you are developing your teaching skills repertoire. You may either fill out the Skills Checklist yourself or ask a teacher to observe you and complete the Skills Checklist for you (peer evaluation). If you are unfamiliar with an item, read about it in the book or talk with your mentor or trainer. The following is an abbreviated checklist related to this module.

_____Teacher uses anecdotal observations to document learning in the classroom. (see pages 19, 21, 228)

_____Teacher has complete and appropriate Possibilities Plan posted in the classroom and uses it to provide activities and experiences for toddlers. (see pages 551-557)

_____Teacher completes forms to document events, progress, and interactions in the classroom. (see pages 18-22, 142, 228, 389, 447-448, 471-472, 536-557)

_____Teacher has periodic conferences with parents using a variety of materials. (see pages 467-472)

_____Teacher plans for and uses Parent Postcards and other resources to support families. (see pages 548-550)

_____Teacher continues growing professionally through reading, training, and professional participation.

_____   _____

Teacher Completing Training Module   Date
(please sign and date)

Congratulations! You have completed Module 37 of 38 in the **Teacher's Guide**.

COMPLETION OF TRAINING

Purpose: to conclude training for *Innovations: The Comprehensive Toddler Curriculum*

TIME: APPROXIMATELY 1 HOUR

Today you will complete the final module in your training for *Innovations: The Comprehensive Toddler Curriculum*. Begin by reviewing this booklet for any additional questions you might have. Read the pages that are referenced and/or discuss your questions with your mentor or trainer.

After you have completed any questions you might have, look back at Module 3 (pages 14-16 in this book). Review your personal goals for training. Do you have any goals that still need to be achieved? List them below. Use the index to look for additional information on topics you still need to explore.

Ask your mentor or trainer to fill in your Certificate of Completion. Post it in your classroom, so parents can see that you have completed your training for *Innovations: The Comprehensive Toddler Curriculum*. Add this training experience to your training records, and place a copy of your certificate of completion in your file.

Skills Checklist

If you are currently in the classroom, use the complete list on page 95 of this book as a frequent skills checklist to confirm that you are developing your teaching skills repertoire. You may either fill out the Skills Checklist yourself or ask a teacher to observe you and complete the Skills Checklist for you (peer evaluation). If you are unfamiliar with an item, read about it in the book or talk with your mentor or trainer. The following is an abbreviated checklist related to this module.

_____Teacher uses anecdotal observations to document learning in the classroom. (see pages 19, 21, 228)

_____Teacher has complete and appropriate Possibilities Plan posted in the classroom and uses it to provide activities and experiences for toddlers. (see pages 551-557)

_____Teacher completes forms to document events, progress, and interactions in the classroom. (see pages 18-22, 142, 228, 389, 447-448, 471-472, 536-557)

_____Teacher plans for and uses Parent Postcards and other resources to support families. (see pages 467-472)

_____Teacher continues growing professionally through reading, training, and other methods.

_____Teacher has copies of the Completion of Training, as well as other credentials, documented and/or posted in the classroom.

_____   _____

Teacher Completing Training Module   Date
(please sign and date)

Congratulations! You have completed Module 38 of 38 in the **Teacher's Guide**.

INNOVATIONS:

COMPLETION OF **41 HOURS** OF TRAINING IN

The Comprehensive Toddler Curriculum

NAME

SCHOOL

DATE

MENTOR or TRAINER

Complete Skills Checklist for Teachers

Use this Skills Checklist for self evaluation, peer evaluation by another teacher, or performance evaluation by your supervisor/director.

_____   _____

Teacher Name   Date

_____Parents and toddlers are greeted warmly. (see pages 45-46)

_____Toys and equipment are disinfected. (see pages 303, 404-405)

_____Diapering procedures are followed. (see pages 385-386)

_____Quality interactions occur during the day. (see pages 294-295)

_____Safety precautions are followed in the classroom (for example, attendance taken, toddlers never left alone, chokeable items eliminated, toys and materials regularly checked for safety). (see page 385)

_____Teacher observes toddlers regularly during the day. (see pages 18-21)

_____Assessment materials are readily available in the classroom (clipboard, pen, forms). (see page 21)

_____Teacher explores and discovers the relationship between behavior and child development principles. (see pages 40-45)

_____Teacher uses routine times to provide individual quality interactions for toddlers. (see page 53)

_____Teacher uses reflection to assess and improve teaching competencies. (see page 23)

_____Teacher supports partnerships with parents through planning and implementing regular parent participation opportunities. (see page 24)

_____Teacher modifies parent participation choices as a result of reflection about the success of planned activities.

_____Teacher creates, maintains, and refreshes appropriate classroom environment. (see pages 67-69)

_____Classroom contains experiences and activities that reflect a wide variety of possibilities for children in the classroom. (see pages 24-29)

_____Teacher uses webbing as a technique to support emergent curriculum. (see page 25)

_____Classroom includes a wide variety of appropriate toys and materials. (see pages 24-29)

_____Classroom includes a variety of safe, appropriate, teacher-made toys. (see page 233)

_____Teacher uses projects to provide repeated experiences over time for toddlers. (see page 29)

_____Teacher plans, implements, and evaluates the success of parent participation activities.

_____Teacher uses Concepts Learned to communicate with parents about their children. (see pages 30-31, 558-569)

_____Teacher identifies resources needed as a part of the planning process.

_____Teacher uses prop boxes to gather, organize, and store appropriate materials for use on particular topics in the classroom. (see page 553)

_____Teacher uses picture files and vocabulary to support children's learning about diversity and emerging literacy skills. (see page 31)

_____Teacher reads to each child every day. (see pages 320-321)

_____Teacher uses rhymes/fingerplays while interacting with toddlers throughout the day. (pages 570-579)

_____Teacher uses music/songs during the day for interaction and to assist with transitions. (see pages 570-579)

_____Teacher uses a system for storing and disinfecting toys and materials. (see pages 157-160)

_____Teacher uses anecdotal observations to document learning in the classroom. (see pages 19, 21, 228)

_____Teacher has complete and appropriate Possibilities Plan posted in the classroom and uses it to provide activities and experiences for toddlers. (see pages 551-557)

_____Teacher completes forms to document events, progress, and interactions in the classroom. (see pages 18-22, 142, 228, 389, 447-448, 471-472, 536-557)

_____Teacher has periodic conferences with parents using a variety of materials. (see pages 467-472)

_____Teacher plans for and uses Parent Postcards and other resources to support families. (see pages 548-550)

_____Teacher continues growing professionally through reading, training, and professional participation.

_____Teacher has copies of the Completion of Training, as well as other credentials, documented and/or posted in the classroom.

Innovations: The Comprehensive Toddler Curriculum

Observation/Assessment
18 to 36 months

Observation/Assessment

CHILD'S NAME   TEACHER

Toddler (18-36 months) Assessment

Task: Transitioning to School

	18-24 months	24-30 months		30-36 months
T1	a. Experienced in separating from Mom and Dad; may resist initial separation in new or unusual settings, but adjusts after a few moments.	b. Experienced with separating; looks forward to favorite activities. May approach new or unusual settings with caution, but gets interested after a few minutes.		c. Separates easily in most situations. If cautious, gets over caution quickly when invited to join in by a friendly adult or peer.
T2	a. Actively seeks new and interesting stimuli; interested in everything in the environment.	b. May get into difficulty seeking and exploring interesting stimuli (e.g., climbing on furniture, opening off-limits cabinets).		c. Seeks novel and interesting stimuli; when presented with familiar and novel stimuli, prefers novel ones.
T3	a. Resists separations and transitions to unfamiliar or new settings or to settings that are not preferred.	b. Transitions to familiar people in familiar settings easily; still cautious about unfamiliar settings or new experiences.		c. Transitions to most settings without distress; when distress occurs, can be comforted or redirected.
T4	a. Separation anxiety begins to resolve; is able to make transitions to familiar settings with familiar adults without experiencing distress. When distress occurs, it resolves when the child gets interested in the new setting and playmates.	b. Stranger anxiety emerges. Fear of strangers and new situations causes proximity-seeking behavior such as getting close to primary caregiver; clinging, crying, resistance of social overtures (e.g, hiding behind adult, hiding face).		c. Stranger anxiety begins resolving; may continue to be cautious, but will accept interactions from strangers after watching or observing for a moment. Takes cues (looks to them, watches their reactions) about new situations from familiar adults.
T5	a. Prefers predictable routines and schedule; manages changes in schedule fairly well at the time but may experience problems later.	b. Ritualistic about routines and schedule—likes routines predictably "just so"; exhibits ritualistic behavior around routines; likes routines the same way every time; needs warnings of anticipated transitions and still may resist them; melts down or tantrums when schedule is changed without reminders and preparation.		c. Adapts to changes in schedule when prepared in advance; abrupt or unplanned schedule changes still present problems; adapts more readily in familiar settings except when tired, hungry, or ill.
T6	a. Tries new food when presented; has strong food preferences.	b. Resists new foods on some days and not on others; reduces intake; may become a picky eater or refuse to try new foods when offered.	c. Has small selection of food preferences; still resists new food when presented; eats well on some days and not on others.	d. Food intake and preferences even out; will try new food after many presentations; needs encouragement to try new foods.
T7	a. Develops a sense of property rights; hoards toys and favorite objects.	b. Considers objects being played with as personal property.		c. Recognizes mine and not mine.

Toddler (18-36 months) Assessment

Task: Making Friends

	18-24 months	24-30 months	30-36 months
MF1	a. Calms self with verbal support from adults and transitional objects.	b. Calms self with verbal support from adults; may look for transitional objects to help with the calm-down process after verbal support is provided. Frequency of emotional outburst begins to diminish.	c. Calms self with only verbal support. Use of transitional objects begins to decline except at bedtime and when recovering from intense emotional outbursts.
MF2	a Goes to mirror to look at self; makes faces and shows emotions such as laughing, crying, and so on.	b. Calls own name when looking at photographs or in the mirror.	c. Calls names of friends in photographs or in the mirror.
MF3	a. Develops preferences for types of play and types of toys.	b. Develops play themes that are repeated again and again (such as mommy or firefighter).	c. Begins exploration of a wider range of play themes. Themes often come from new experiences.
MF4	a. Perfects gross motor skills such as running, climbing, and riding push toys. Fine motor skills with manipulatives (simple puzzles, Duplos, and so on) are emerging.	b. Likes physical challenges such as running fast, jumping high, and going up and down stairs. Plays with preferred manipulatives for increasing periods of time.	c. Competently exhibits a wide range of physical skills. Begins to be interested in practicing skills such as throwing a ball, riding a tricycle, or completing a puzzle.
MF5	a. Play may be onlooker, solitary, or parallel in nature.	b. Play is predominantly parallel in nature.	c. Exhibits associative play with familiar play partners.
MF6	a. Exhibits symbolic play.	b. Practices and explores a wide variety of symbolic play themes and roles.	
MF7	a. Objects to strangers' presence; clings, cries, and seeks support when strangers are around.	b. Objection to strangers begins to diminish; may still be wary of strangers or new situations.	c. Is able to venture into strange or new situations if prepared in advance and supported by adults.
MF8	a. Uses single words to indicate needs and wants such as "muk" for "I want milk," or "bye bye" for "Let's go bye bye."	b. Uses phrases and 2- to 3-word sentences to indicate needs and wants.	c. Uses 4- to 6-word sentences to indicate needs and wants.

	18-24 months	24-30 months		30-36 months
MF9	a. Connects emotions with behaviors; uses language to express these connections.	b. Uses emotional ideas in play.	c. Elaborates on emotional ideas and understanding to play with objects.	d. Begins emotional thinking; begins to understand emotional cause-and-effect relationships.

	18-24 months	24-36 months		
MF10	a. Takes turns with toys and materials with adult support and facilitation.	b. Takes turns with toys and materials with friend, sometimes without adult support.		
MF11	a. Experiments with behavior that accomplishes a goal; may bite, pinch, poke, scratch, push, and so on while trying to make things happen.	b. Begins to anticipate what might happen when actions are taken; chooses to make things happen if outcomes are desirable (e.g., trade toys with a friend who will stay and play), and resists taking action if outcomes are undesirable (e.g., teacher putting markers away if child chews on the tips).		

Toddler (18-36 months) Assessment

Task: Exploring Roles

	18-24 months	24-30 months	30-36 months
ER1	a. Explores roles related to self and family.	b. Explores roles related to self, friends, family, and neighborhood.	c. Explores roles related to self, friends, family, neighborhood, and the community at large.
ER2	a. Is unable to choose or modify behavior in response to physical or social cues of situations; persists in using behavior that doesn't work in situations.	b. Begins to choose or modify behavior in response to physical and social cues of situations; when one behavior isn't working, may stop and try something else.	c. Chooses and modifies behavior in response to the physical and social cues of a situation; tries to choose the behaviors that will get what he or she wants; can change behaviors if they are not working.
ER3	a. Does not understand the impact of own behavior on others.	b. Begins to understand the impact of own behavior on others; shows interest and awareness of the emotional behaviors of friends and others.	c. Understands the impact of own behavior on others; anticipates how friends or others will react.
ER4	a. Uses props to play roles; becomes the occupant of the role (e.g., is superman when wearing a cape or mommy when holding a baby). Prefers familiar roles.	b. Uses props to adopt roles; abandons roles when the props are removed; changes between familiar and favorite roles in dramatic play.	c. Can play roles with or without props. Transitions between roles frequently and easily (e.g., can be the mommy, then the daddy, then the monster during same play period).

Toddler (18-36 months) Assessment

Task: *Communicating with Parents, Teachers, and Friends*

	18-24 months		24-30 months	30-36 months
CM1	a. Expressive vocabulary increases; uses about 200 words on a regular basis. Expressive language continues to be telegraphic, where single words may carry expanded meaning only understood by familiar caregivers.		b. Vocabulary size begins to grow rapidly; sentence length begins to increase with 3 or 4 words in some sentences.	c. Sentence length continues to grow. Four- to six-word sentences predominate expressive language. Vocabulary continues to expand; expressive vocabulary is adequate to make most needs and wants understood by others.
CM2	a. Uses a greater variety of sounds and sound combinations, simplifying the word if it is too complex (such as pane for plane, tephone for telephone); enjoys experimenting with inflection that sounds like adult speech although it is not yet understandable.		b. Rapid development of new sound combinations and new words that are understandable to adults. Uses language functionally— to ask for things and get needs met and to interact with friends.	c. Is able to use language to get most needs and wants met by familiar caregivers and to interact with friends.
CM3	a. Seeks vocal interactions with familiar people; can communicate needs and wants to familiar caregivers; begins to be wary of talking to strangers.		b. Resists interactions with strangers; hides, withdraws, or objects to encouragement to talk to strangers.	
CM4	a. 20-25% of language is intelligible to strangers. Parents and caregivers can understand more.		b. 60-65% of language is intelligible to strangers. Parents and caregivers understand most of the child's expressive language.	
CM5	a. "Reads" book from front to back; turns books right side up to look at them.	b. Makes sounds that connect to pictures in books.	c. Listens to a complete story from beginning to end; asks to read familiar books over and over again.	d. Likes to look at books independently; "reads" books to self.
CM6	a. Actively experiments with the environment; follows visual displacement of objects.		b. Begins transition to symbolic thought. Uses formed mental images to solve problems. Thought processes relate to concrete experiences and objects.	c. Begins transition to pre-operational stage characterized by the beginning of symbolic thought and the use of mental images and words.

Toddler (18-36 months) Assessment

Task: Problem-solving

	18-24 months	24-30 months	30-36 months
PS1	a. Interest in toileting is limited to watching; may show interest in flushing toilet, sitting on the toilet, or washing hands. Interest may wax and wane quickly.	b. Toilet play stage of toileting; interested in playing at toileting activities such as taking off diaper, sitting on the toilet, using toilet paper, flushing the toilet, and washing hands.	c. Toilet practice begins; likes to repeat toileting activities again and again, with or without success.
PS2	a. Activity level increases; requests and seeks out motor activities. Does not control activity level without adult support; yet resists adult support in modulating activity level.	b. Activity level continues to increase; continues to seek out motor activities. Begins to modulate activity levels with verbal and physical adult support (e.g, slow down, take a deep breath).	c. Alternates between high levels of activity and periods of calm, quieter activity. Can modulate activity level with verbal reminders from adults.
PS3	a. On-task behavior begins to increase.	b. Able to sustain favorite activities for increasingly longer periods of time; extends on-task play time at favorite activities to 10 minutes. Still loses interest in other activities quickly.	c. Stays on task at favorite manipulative activities for sustained periods of time; extends on-task play time at favorite activities to 20 minutes. Still loses interest in other activities quickly.
PS4	a. Carries toys around from place to place.	b. Undresses; takes off shoes, socks, and clothes.	c. Turns door knob to open door.	d. Holds cup with one hand to drink.	e. Shows preference for one hand.	f. Unzips zipper.	g. Pulls pants up.	h. Zips zipper.
PS5	a. Propels riding toys with feet.	b. Runs; collapses to stop forward movement.	c. Goes up stairs without alternating feet, holding on to handrail.	d. Runs; begins to control starting and stopping.	e. Balances on one foot.	f. Goes up stairs alternating feet, holding on to handrail.	g. Jumps up and down on two feet.	h. Pedals tricycle.

Toddler (18-36 months) Assessment

Task: Expressing Feelings with Parents, Teachers, and Friends

	18-24 months		24-30 months	30-36 months	
E1	a. Begins to create mental images of emotional behaviors.	b. Uses behavior to express emotions (e.g., stomps foot).	c. Distinguishes between emotions and the behaviors that go with that emotion (e.g., feeling mad vs. acting mad).	d. Understands how one feeling relates to another (e.g., being disappointed about getting a toy and getting angry as a result of the disappointment).	
E2	a. Emotional intensity is not regulated—minor and major events get similar reactions; falls apart easily.		b. Begins to regulate emotional intensity in some situations; falls apart less frequently.	c. Regulates emotional intensity most of the time; seldom falls apart.	d. Figures out how to respond with appropriate emotions to most situations.
E3	a. Watches and remembers emotional behaviors exhibited by others; uses observations in future interactions.		b. Puts emotional mental images to work in pretend play; can make-believe or pretend to be angry, happy, sad, and so on.		
E4	a. Knows rules that have been reinforced consistently but still needs reminders and physical adult support to comply.		b. Follows rules that have been reinforced consistently with verbal reminders and physical adult support.	c. Follows rules that have been reinforced consistently with just verbal reminders.	
E5	a. Unable to label own feelings.		b. Can label some feelings; uses the same feeling to represent many feelings (e.g., mad for angry, frustrated, irritated, unhappy, etc.).	c. Labels most of his or her own feelings; can differentiate between similar emotions and label them appropriately.	
E6	a. Unable to understand how others feel.		b. Begins to understand how others feel when observing others but not when he or she is a part of the interaction.	c. Understands how others feel when the behavior exhibited is consistent with the emotion being felt (e.g., angry child is yelling, stomping foot, saying, "No!").	
E7	a. Has difficulty delaying gratification.		b. Can delay gratification for a short time when supported by adults.	c. Can delay gratification for a few minutes in most situations.	
E8	a. Does not separate fantasy from reality.		b. Can switch from reality to fantasy.	c. Understands "real" and "not real."	
E9	a. Ambivalent about being autonomous; wants to sometimes and doesn't want to at other times.		b. Independent behaviors are increasing; dependent behaviors are decreasing.	c. Independent behaviors are usually present.	
E10	a. Has little control over impulses.		b. Controls impulses in some situations or with support from adults.	c. Most impulses are under control.	
E11	a. Loses emotional control often and intensely.		b. Loss of emotional control is less frequent, less intense, and less prolonged.	c. Infrequently loses emotional control.	

Toddler (18-36 months) Observation and Assessment Summary

	18-24 months		24-30 months		30-36 months	
	Subtask	Date	Subtask	Date	Subtask	Date
Task 1 **Transitioning to** **School**	T1a		T1b		T1c	
	T2a		T2b		T2c	
	T3a		T3b		T3c	
			T3c			
	T4a		T4b		T4c	
	T5a		T5b		T5c	
	T6a		T6b		T6d	
			T6c			
	T7a		T7b		T7c	
Task 2 **Making Friends**	MF1a		MF1b		MF1c	
	MF2a		MF2b		MF2c	
	MF3a		MF3b		MF3c	
	MF4a		MF4b		MF4c	
	MF5a		MF5b		MF5c	
	MF6a		MF6b		MF6b	
	MF7a		MF7b		MF7c	
	MF8a		MF8b		MF8c	
	MF9a		MF9b		MF9d	
			MF9c			
	MF10a		MF10b		MF10b	
	MF11a		MF11b		MF11b	
Task 3 **Exploring Roles**	ER1a		ER1b		ER1c	
	ER2a		ER2b		ER2c	
	ER3a		ER3b		ER3c	
	ER4a		ER4b		ER4c	
Task 4 **Communicating with** **Parents, Teachers, and** **Friends**	CM1a		CM1b		CM1c	
	CM2a		CM2b		CM2c	
	CM3a		CM3b		CM3b	
	CM4a		CM4b		CM4b	
	CM5a		CM5c		CM5d	
	CM5b					
	CM6a		CM6b		CM6c	

	18-24 months		24-30 months		30-36 months	
	Subtask	Date	Subtask	Date	Subtask	Date
Task 5 **Problem-solving**	PS1a		PS1b		PS1c	
	PS2a		PS2b		PS2c	
	PS3a		PS3b		PS3c	
	PS4a		PS4d		PS4f	
	PS4b		PS4e		PS4g	
	PS4c				PS4h	
	PS5a		PS5c		PS5f	
	PS5b		PS5d		PS5g	
			PS5e		PS5h	
Task 6 **Expressing Feelings** **with Parents,** **Teachers, and Friends**	E1a		E1c		E1d	
	E1b					
	E2a		E2b		E2c	
					E2d	
	E3a		E3b		E3b	
	E4a		E4b		E4c	
	E5a		E5b		E5c	
	E6a		E6b		E6c	
	E7a		E7b		E7c	
	E8a		E8b		E8c	
	E9a		E9b		E9c	
	E10a		E10b		E10c	
	E11a		E11b		E11c	

Possibilities

Parent Possibilities

Teacher-Initiated

Parent Participation

Innovations in Environments

Observation/Assessment Possibilities

Interactive Experiences

Plan

INNOVATIONS

Web

Dramatic Possibilities

Art/Sensory Possibilities

Curiosity Possibilities

Construction Possibilities

Music/Movement Possibilities

Literacy Possibilities

Outdoor Possibilities

Project Possibilities

Books	Picture File Pictures/Vocabulary

Rhymes & Fingerplays	Music/Songs	Prop Boxes

Anecdotal Record

Child _____ Date _____ Time _____

What I observed _____

_____

_____

_____

_____

_____

_____

_____

_____

Teacher _____

Anecdotal Record

Child _____ Date _____ Time _____

What I observed _____

_____

_____

_____

_____

_____

_____

_____

_____

_____

Teacher _____

Books Read List

Book Title	Date
1.	
2.	
3.	
4.	
5.	
6.	
7.	
8.	
9.	
10.	
11.	
12.	
13.	
14.	
15.	
16.	
17.	
18.	
19.	
20.	
21.	
22.	
23.	
24.	
25.	
26.	
27.	
28.	
29.	
30.	

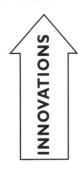

Communication Sheet

CHILD'S NAME _____ **FOR THE WEEK OF** _____

DAY	BREAKFAST	TOTAL HOURS SLEPT	BEHAVIOR CHANGES NOTICED	PARENT COMMENTS/INSTRUCTIONS	FOODS EATEN — SOLIDS	FOODS EATEN — LIQUIDS	DIAPER CHANGES — WET	DIAPER CHANGES — BM	NAPTIME — START	NAPTIME — WOKE	TEACHER COMMENTS
M	YES / NO		YES / NO								
T	YES / NO		YES / NO								
W	YES / NO		YES / NO								
Th	YES / NO		YES / NO								
F	YES / NO		YES / NO								

Parent Visit Log

School Name _____

Date	Name of Parent
1.	
2.	
3.	
4.	
5.	
6.	
7.	
8.	
9.	
10.	
11.	
12.	
13.	
14.	
15.	
16.	
17.	
18.	
19.	
20.	
21.	
22.	
23.	
24.	
25.	
26.	
27.	
28.	
29.	
30.	

Accident/Incident Report
(for school records)

Name of injured child

Date of accident/incident

Location of accident (address)

Site (place in school)

What happened? Describe what took place.

Why did it happen? Give all of the facts—why? where? what? when? who? etc.

What should be done to prevent this accident from recurring?

If the accident involved a child, how were the parents notified and by whom?

What was the parent's reaction?

What has been done so far to correct the situation?

With whom was this accident discussed, other than the child's parents?

Reported by   Date

HELPFUL HINTS FOR COMPLETING OBSERVATIONS AND ASSESSMENTS

Plan to observe regularly, but don't overlook daily observations that occur in real time. If you note a new skill or play interest, write it on the Communication Sheet so you won't forget it and attach a copy of the Communication Sheet to the assessment. Use these "real time" observations to support formal observations.

Take anecdotal notes as you observe. Notes can be about one child, or about more than one child. If you record information about more than one child, copy the note and file it in both children's files.

After taking anecdotal notes, look at the appropriate assessment to determine if you observed any of the assessment items listed. If you did, simply date the assessment item, indicating that you have an anecdotal note that documents your observation of the skill (i.e., Anecdotal Note, 3/3/00 or AN 3/30/00).

Put the date ranges for the child on the chart below the age ranges to cue you to the child's birthdate and confirm you are observing the right sections.

Look for secondary sources for some assessment items. For example, check Communication Sheets, Books Read Lists, word lists, anecdotal notes, and any other sources of information to see if you can confirm the presence of skills from these sources.

If you don't observe an item during the time range of the skill, and subsequent skills are noted, put "not observed (N/O)" in the date space.

Toddler (18-36 months) Assessment

Task: Transitioning to School

	18-24 months 6/29/00 – 12/29/00	24-30 months 12/29/00 – 6/29/01	30-36 months 6/29/01 – 12/29/01
T1	a. Experienced in separating from Mom and Dad; may resist initial separation in new or unusual settings, but adjusts after a few moments. 7/16/00	b. Experienced with separating; looks forward to favorite activities. May approach new or unusual settings with caution, but gets interested after a few minutes. 3/10/01	c. Separates easily in most situations. If cautious, gets over caution quickly when invited to join in by a friendly adult or peer.
T2	a. Actively seeks new and interesting stimuli; interested in everything in the environment. 6/15/00	b. May get into difficulty seeking and exploring interesting stimuli (e.g., climbing on furniture, opening off-limits cabinets).　1/2/01	c. Seeks novel and interesting stimuli; when presented with familiar and novel stimuli, prefers novel ones.　4/8/01
T3	a. Resists separations and transitions to unfamiliar or new settings or to settings that are not preferred.　10/10/00	b. Transitions to familiar people in familiar settings easily; still cautious about unfamiliar settings or new experiences.　6/6/01	c. Transitions to most settings without distress; when distress occurs, can be comforted or redirected.
T4	a. Separation anxiety begins to resolve; is able to make transitions to familiar settings with familiar adults without experiencing distress. When distress occurs, it resolves when the child gets interested in the new setting and playmates.　12/5/00	b. Stranger anxiety emerges. Fear of strangers and new situations causes proximity-seeking behavior such as getting close to primary caregiver; clinging, crying, resistance of social overtures (e.g, hiding behind adult, hiding face).　7/15/01	c. Stranger anxiety begins resolving; may continue to be cautious, but will accept interactions from strangers after watching or observing for a moment. Takes cues (looks to them, watches their reactions) about new situations from familiar adults.　10/10/01
T5	a. Prefers predictable routines and schedule; manages changes in schedule fairly well at the time but may experience problems later. 12/11/00	b. Ritualistic about routines and schedule—likes routines predictably "just so"; exhibits ritualistic behavior around routines; likes routines the same way every time; needs warnings of anticipated transitions and still may resist them; melts down or tantrums when schedule is changed without reminders and preparation.　7/20/01	c. Adapts to changes in schedule when prepared in advance; abrupt or unplanned schedule changes still present problems; adapts more readily in familiar settings except when tired, hungry, or ill.

T6	a. Tries new food when presented; has strong food preferences. 7/16/00	b. Resists new foods on some days and not on others; reduces intake; may become a picky eater or refuse to try new foods when offered. 9/10/00	c. Has small selection of food preferences; still resists new food when presented; eats well on some days and not on others. 3/15/01	d. Food intake and preferences even out; will try new food after many presentations; needs encouragement to try new foods.

T7	a. Develops a sense of property rights; hoards toys and favorite objects. 10/10/00	b. Considers objects being played with as personal property.　7/20/01	c. Recognizes mine and not mine.　9/10/01

Toddler (18-36 months) Assessment

Task: Making Friends

	18-24 months 6/29/00 – 12/29/00	24-30 months 12/29/00 – 6/29/01	30-36 months 6/29/01 – 12/29/01
MF1	a. Calms self with verbal support from adults and transitional objects. 7/3/00	b. Calms self with verbal support from adults; may look for transitional objects to help with the calm-down process after verbal support is provided. Frequency of emotional outburst begins to diminish. AN 5/14/01	c. Calms self with only verbal support. Use of transitional objects begins to decline except at bedtime and when recovering from intense emotional outbursts. 10/18/01
MF2	a Goes to mirror to look at self; makes faces, and shows emotions such as laughing, crying, and so on. 7/16/00	b. Calls own name when looking at photographs or in the mirror. 7/16/01	c. Calls names of friends in photographs or in the mirror. 4/8/01
MF3	a. Develops preferences for types of play and types of toys. 6/15/00	b. Develops play themes that are repeated again and again (such as mommy or firefighter). *Loves to play grocery store* 8/4/01	c. Begins exploration of a wider range of play themes. Themes often come from new experiences.
MF4	a. Perfects gross motor skills such as running, climbing, and riding push toys. Fine motor skills with manipulatives (simple puzzles, Duplos, and so on) are emerging.	b. Likes physical challenges such as running fast, jumping high, and going up and down stairs. Plays with preferred manipulatives for increasing periods of time.	c. Competently exhibits a wide range of physical skills. Begins to be interested in practicing skills such as throwing a ball, riding a tricycle, or completing a puzzle.
MF5	a. Play may be onlooker, solitary, or parallel in nature. AN 6/15/00	b. Play is predominantly parallel in nature. 11/30/00	c. Exhibits associative play with familiar play partners. 6/1/01 Paula/Sophie
MF6	a. Exhibits symbolic play. 6/29/00	b. Practices and explores a wide variety of symbolic play themes and roles.	
MF7	a. Objects to strangers' presence; clings, cries, and seeks support when strangers are around.	b. Objection to strangers begins to diminish; may still be wary of strangers or new situations.	c. Is able to venture into strange or new situations if prepared in advance and supported by adults.
MF8	a. Uses single words to indicate needs and wants such as "muk" for "I want milk," or "bye bye" for "Let's go bye bye." *"More Milk"* 6/30/00	b. Uses phrases and 2- to 3-word sentences to indicate needs and wants. *"Don't touch my toy!"* 2/6/01	c. Uses 4- to 6-word sentences to indicate needs and wants.

	18-24 months	24-30 months	30-36 months
MF9	a. Connects emotions with behaviors; uses language to express these connections. 11/11/00 *"Pretends" to cry, then looks to see who noticed!*	b. Uses emotional ideas in play. 3/7/01 Crashes blocks together and says they are 'mad at each other.	c. Elaborates on emotional ideas and 3/7/01 understanding to play with objects.	d. Begins emotional thinking; begins to understand emotional cause-and-effect relationships. 7/13/01 *"When is mommy coming to get me?"*
MF10	a. Takes turns with toys and materials with adult support and facilitation. 6/29/00	b. Takes turns with toys and materials with friend, sometimes without adult support. AN 5/31/01; 9/16/01		
MF11	a. Experiments with behavior that accomplishes a goal; may bite, pinch, poke, scratch, push, and so on while trying to make things happen. AN 9/28/00	b. Begins to anticipate what might happen when actions are taken; chooses to make things happen if outcomes are desirable (e.g., trade toys with a friend who will stay and play), and resists taking action if outcomes are undesirable (e.g., teacher putting markers away if child chews on the tips). AN 5/31/01, AN 9/16/01		

Toddler (18-36 months) Assessment

Task: Exploring Roles

	18-24 months 6/29/00 – 12/29/00	24-30 months 12/29/00 – 6/29/01	30-36 months 6/29/01 – 12/29/01
ER1	a. Explores roles related to self and family. *Loves to play mommy.* *6/29/00*	b. Explores roles related to self, friends, family, and neighborhood. *AN 4/16/01*	c. Explores roles related to self, friends, family, neighborhood, and the community at large. *AN 7/16/01*
ER2	a. Is unable to choose or modify behavior in response to physical or social cues of situations; persists in using behavior that doesn't work in situations. *7/21/00* *Cries for cookies or snack, even after snack time is over.*	b. Begins to choose or modify behavior in response to physical and social cues of situations; when one behavior isn't working, may stop and try something else. *AN 4/16/01*	c. Chooses and modifies behavior in response to the physical and social cues of a situation; tries to choose the behaviors that will get what he or she wants; can change behaviors if they are not working.
ER3	a. Does not understand the impact of own behavior on others. *Tries to hold Maddie's hand. Persists when Maddie hides her hand behind her back. 9/11/00*	b. Begins to understand the impact of own behavior on others; shows interest and awareness of the emotional behaviors of friends and others. *Offers pacifier to friend when hurt on playground. 3/1/01*	c. Understands the impact of own behavior on others; anticipates how friends or others will react.
ER4	a. Uses props to play roles; becomes the occupant of the role (e.g., is superman when wearing a cape or mommy when holding a baby). Prefers familiar roles. *Loves firefighter prop box. Plays with Seth as co-firefighter. 8/30/00*	b. Uses props to adopt roles; abandons roles when the props are removed; changes between familiar and favorite roles in dramatic play. *Favorite roles include firefighter, Mommy, big sister, and Choir Director. 1/29/01*	c. Can play roles with or without props. Transitions between roles frequently and easily (e.g., can be the mommy, then the daddy, then the monster during same play period). *AN 7/16/01*

Toddler (18-36 months) Assessment

Task: *Communicating with Parents, Teachers, and Friends*

	18-24 months 6/29/00 – 12/29/00	24-30 months 12/29/00 – 6/29/01	30-36 months 6/29/01 – 12/29/01
CM1	a. Expressive vocabulary increases; uses about 200 words on a regular basis. Expressive language continues to be telegraphic, where single words may carry expanded meaning only understood by familiar caregivers. *See voc. list.*	b. Vocabulary size begins to grow rapidly; sentence length begins to increase with 3 or 4 words in some sentences. *See sample sentences in portfolios.*	c. Sentence length continues to grow. Four- to six-word sentences predominate expressive language. Vocabulary continues to expand; expressive vocabulary is adequate to make most needs and wants understood by others. *7-word sentences 9/30/01*
CM2	a. Uses a greater variety of sounds and sound combinations, simplifying the word if it is too complex (such as pane for plane, tephone for telephone); enjoys experimenting with inflection that sounds like adult speech although it is not yet understandable. *ninga=pacifier 6/29/00*	b. Rapid development of new sound combinations and new words that are understandable to adults. Uses language functionally— to ask for things and get needs met and to interact with friends. *2/14/01*	c. Is able to use language to get most needs and wants met by familiar caregivers and to interact with friends. *8/14/01*
CM3	a. Seeks vocal interactions with familiar people; can communicate needs and wants to familiar caregivers; begins to be wary of talking to strangers. *6/29/00*	b. Resists interactions with strangers; hides, withdraws, or objects to encouragement to talk to strangers. *See An 2/14/01; 5/29/01*	
CM4	a. 20-25% of language is intelligible to strangers. Parents and caregivers can understand more. *6/29/00*	b. 60-65% of language is intelligible to strangers. Parents and caregivers understand most of the child's expressive language. *At least 60-65% on 5/29/01*	
CM5	a. "Reads" book from front to back; turns books right side up to look at them. *7/1/00* b. Makes sounds that connect to pictures in books. *7/1/00*	c. Listens to a complete story from beginning to end; asks to read familiar books over and over again. *12/29/00*	d. Likes to look at books independently; "reads" books to self. *6/29/01* *See Books Read List*
CM6	a. Actively experiments with the environment; follows visual displacement of objects. *7/17/00*	b. Begins transition to symbolic thought. Uses formed mental images to solve problems. Thought processes relate to concrete experiences and objects. *4/16/01*	c. Begins transition to pre-operational stage characterized by the beginning of symbolic thought and the use of mental images and words.

Toddler (18-36 months) Assessment

Task: Problem-solving

	18-24 months 6/29/00 – 12/29/00	24-30 months 12/29/00 – 6/29/01	30-36 months 6/29/01 – 12/29/01
PS1	a. Interest in toileting is limited to watching; may show interest in flushing toilet, sitting on the toilet, or washing hands. Interest may wax and wane quickly. 10/15/00	b. Toilet play stage of toileting; interested in playing at toileting activities such as taking off diaper; sitting on the toilet, using toilet paper, flushing the toilet, and washing hands. 3/17/01	c. Toilet practice begins; likes to repeat toileting activities again and again, with or without success.
PS2	a. Activity level increases; requests and seeks out motor activities. Does not control activity level without adult support; yet resists adult support in modulating activity level. 7/29/00	b. Activity level continues to increase; continues to seek out motor activities. Begins to modulate activity levels with verbal and physical adult support (e.g, slow down, take a deep breath). 4/21/01	c. Alternates between high levels of activity and periods of calm, quieter activity. Can modulate activity level with verbal reminders from adults.
PS3	a. On-task behavior begins to increase. 9/30/00 Played with Suzette in Dramatic Possibilities for 18 minutes.	b. Able to sustain favorite activities for increasingly longer periods of time; extends on-task play time at favorite activities to 10 minutes. Still loses interest in other activities quickly. 12/29/00 – 7 minutes 3/1/01 – 17 minutes	c. Stays on task at favorite manipulative activities for sustained periods of time; extends on-task play time at favorite activities to 20 minutes. Still loses interest in other activities quickly. 3/29/01 – 20 minutes 6/1/01 – 20 minutes
PS4	a. Carries toys around from place to place. No / b. Undresses; takes off shoes, socks, and clothes. No / c. Turns door knob to open door. Tried 6/30/00 Perfected 8/30/00	d. Holds cup with one hand to drink. 12/1/00 / e. Shows preference for one hand. 3/11/01	f. Unzips zipper. / g. Pulls pants up. / h. Zips zipper.
PS5	a. Propels riding toys with feet. 6/29/00 / b. Runs; collapses to stop forward movement.	c. Goes up stairs without alternating feet, holding on to handrail. 11/6/00 / d. Runs; begins to control starting and stopping. 12/1/00 / e. Balances on one foot. 3/11/01	f. Goes up stairs alternating feet, holding on to handrail. 3/17/01 / g. Jumps up and down on two feet. / h. Pedals tricycle.

Toddler (18-36 months) Assessment

Task: Expressing Feelings with Parents, Teachers, and Friends

	18-24 months 6/29/00 – 12/29/00		24-30 months 12/29/00 – 6/29/01	30-36 months 6/29/01 – 12/29/01	
E1	a. Begins to create mental images of emotional behaviors. 10/11/00	b. Uses behavior to express emotions (e.g., stomps foot). 10/11/00	c. Distinguishes between emotions and the behaviors that go with that emotion (e.g., feeling mad vs. acting mad). 3/16/01	d. Understands how one feeling relates to another (e.g., being disappointed about getting a toy and getting angry as a result of the disappointment).	
E2	a. Emotional intensity is not regulated—minor and major events get similar reactions; falls apart easily. AN 7/15/00		b. Begins to regulate emotional intensity in some situations; falls apart less frequently. AN 7/10/00	c. Regulates emotional intensity most of the time; seldom falls apart.	d. Figures out how to respond with appropriate emotions to most situations.
E3	a. Watches and remembers emotional behaviors exhibited by others; uses observations in future interactions. Copied Daniel's play with tractors and farm animals. 9/26/00		b. Puts emotional mental images to work in pretend play; can make-believe or pretend to be angry, happy, sad, and so on. AN 5/14/01		
E4	a. Knows rules that have been reinforced consistently but still needs reminders and physical adult support to comply. 6/29/00		b. Follows rules that have been reinforced consistently with verbal reminders and physical adult support. 11/15/00	c. Follows rules that have been reinforced consistently with just verbal reminders.	
E5	a. Unable to label own feelings. 10/11/00		b. Can label some feelings; uses the same feeling to represent many feelings (e.g., mad for angry, frustrated, irritated, unhappy, etc.). AN 5/14/01	c. Labels most of his or her own feelings; can differentiate between similar emotions and label them appropriately.	
E6	a. Unable to understand how others feel. AN 6/15/00		b. Begins to understand how others feel when observing others but not when he or she is a part of the interaction. AN 5/14/01	c. Understands how others feel when the behavior exhibited is consistent with the emotion being felt (e.g., angry child is yelling, stomping foot, saying, "No!").	
E7	a. Has difficulty delaying gratification. 6/29/00		b. Can delay gratification for a short time when supported by adults. 3/16/01	c. Can delay gratification for a few minutes in most situations.	
E8	a. Does not separate fantasy from reality. 7/15/00		b. Can switch from reality to fantasy. 5/29/01	c. Understands "real" and "not real."	
E9	a. Ambivalent about being autonomous; wants to sometimes and doesn't want to at other times.		b. Independent behaviors are increasing; dependent behaviors are decreasing. 3/16/01	c. Independent behaviors are usually present.	
E10	a. Has little control over impulses. AN 10/11/00		b. Controls impulses in some situations or with support from adults. 8/26/01	c. Most impulses are under control.	
E11	a. Loses emotional control often and intensely. AN 6/15/00		b. Loss of emotional control is less frequent, less intense, and less prolonged. 3/16/01	c. Infrequently loses emotional control.	

Toddler (18-36 months) Observation and Assessment Summary

	18-24 months		24-30 months		30-36 months	
	Subtask	Date	Subtask	Date	Subtask	Date
Task 1 Transitioning to School	T1a	7/16/00	T1b	3/10/01	T1c	
	T2a	6/15/00	T2b	1/2/01	T2c	4/8/01
	T3a	10/10/00	T3b	6/6/01	T3c	
	T4a	12/5/00	T4b	7/15/01	T4c	10/10/01
	T5a	12/11/00	T5b	7/20/01	T5c	
	T6a	7/16/00	T6b	9/10/00	T6d	
			T6c	3/15/01		
	T7a	10/10/00	T7b	7/20/01	T7c	9/10/01
Task 2 Making Friends	MF1a	7/3/00	MF1b	5/14/01	MF1c	10/18/01
	MF2a	7/16/00	MF2b	7/16/00	MF2c	4/8/01
	MF3a	6/15/00	MF3b	8/4/01	MF3c	
	MF4a		MF4b		MF4c	
	MF5a	6/15/00	MF5b	11/30/00	MF5c	6/1/01
	MF6a	6/29/00	MF6b		MF6b	
	MF7a		MF7b		MF7c	
	MF8a	6/30/00	MF8b	2/6/01	MF8c	
	MF9a	11/11/00	MF9b	3/7/01	MF9d	7/13/01
			MF9c	3/7/01		
	MF10a	6/29/00	MF10b	5/31/01	MF10b	9/16/01
	MF11a	9/28/00	MF11b	5/31/01	MF11b	9/16/01
Task 3 Exploring Roles	ER1a	6/29/00	ER1b	4/16/01	ER1c	7/16/01
	ER2a	7/21/00	ER2b	4/16/01	ER2c	
	ER3a	9/11/00	ER3b	3/1/01	ER3c	
	ER4a	8/30/00	ER4b	1/29/01	ER4c	7/16/01
Task 4 Communicating with Parents, Teachers, and Friends	CM1a	see voc list	CM1b		CM1c	9/30/01
	CM2a	6/29/00	CM2b	2/14/01	CM2c	8/14/01
	CM3a	6/29/00	CM3b	2/14/01	CM3b	5/29/01
	CM4a	6/29/00	CM4b	5/29/01	CM4b	
	CM5a	7/1/00	CM5c	12/29/00	CM5d	6/29/01
	CM5b	7/1/00				
	CM6a	7/17/00	CM6b	4/6/01	CM6c	

Toddler (18-36 months) Observation and Assessment Summary (continued)

	18-24 months		24-30 months		30-36 months	
	Subtask	Date	Subtask	Date	Subtask	Date
Task 5 **Problem-solving**	PS1a	10/15/00	PS1b	2/17/01	PS1c	
	PS2a	7/29/00	PS2b	4/21/01	PS2c	
	PS3a	9/30/00	PS3b	12/29/00	PS3c	3/29/01
	PS4a		PS4d	12/11/00	PS4f	
	PS4b		PS4e	3/11/01	PS4g	
	PS4c	6/30/00			PS4h	
	PS5a	6/29/00	PS5c	11/6/00	PS5f	
	PS5b	7/16/00	PS5d	12/1/00	PS5g	
			PS5e	3/17/01	PS5h	
Task 6 **Expressing Feelings** **with Parents,** **Teachers, and Friends**	E1a	10/11/00	E1c	3/16/01	E1d	
	E1b	10/11/00				
	E2a	7/15/00	E2b	7/10/00	E2c	
					E2d	
	E3a	9/16/00	E3b	5/14/01	E3b	
	E4a	6/29/00	E4b	11/15/00	E4c	
	E5a	10/11/00	E5b	5/14/01	E5c	
	E6a	6/15/00	E6b	5/14/01	E6c	
	E7a	6/29/00	E7b	3/16/01	E7c	
	E8a	7/15/00	E8b	5/29/01	E8c	
	E9a		E9b	3/16/01	E9c	
	E10a	10/11/00	E10b	8/26/01	E10c	
	E11a	6/15/00	E11b	3/16/01	E11c	

Index

Innovations

Kay Albrecht and Linda G. Miller

Everything you need for a complete infant and toddler program.The *Innovations* curriculum series is a comprehensive, interactive curriculum for infants and toddlers. Responding to children's interests is at the heart of emergent curriculum and central to the *Innovations* series, which meets the full spectrum of needs for teachers, parents, and the children they care for. In addition to the wealth of activities, each book includes these critical components:

- Applying child development theory to everyday experiences
- Using assessment to meet individual developmental needs of infants and toddlers
- Using the physical environment as a learning tool
- Developing a partner relationship with parents
- Fostering an interactive climate in the classroom
- Educating parents

The *Innovations* series is a unique combination of the practical and theoretical. It combines them in a way that provides support for beginning teachers, information for experienced teachers, and a complete program for every teacher!

Innovations: The Comprehensive Infant Curriculum

416 pages

ISBN 0-87659-213-2 / Gryphon House / 14962 / $39.95

Innovations: The Comprehensive Toddler Curriculum

416 pages

ISBN 0-87659-214-0 / Gryphon House / 17846 / $39.95

Available at your favorite bookstore, school supply store, or order directly from
Gryphon House at 800.638.0928 or www.gryphon house.com

Innovations: Infant & Toddler Development

Kay Albrecht and Linda G. Miller

Understanding infant and toddler behavior can be a challenge. But this *Innovations* book provides teachers with a more thorough understanding of the knowledge base that informs early childhood practice. Focusing on the development of children from birth to age three, *Innovations: Infant and Toddler Development* gives you an in-depth guide to the underlying ages and stages, theories, and best practices of the early childhood field. This enables teachers to begin to address these challenging behaviors in developmentally appropriate ways. 372 pages.

ISBN 0-87659-259-0 / Gryphon House / 19237 / PB / $39.95

Innovations: The Comprehensive Infant & Toddler Curriculum
A Trainer's Guide

Linda G. Miller and Kay Albrecht

The tool every administrator, director, or program manager needs to provide comprehensive training for infant and toddler teachers who are using the *Innovations series (Innovations: The Comprehensive Infant Curriculum* and *Innovations: The Comprehensive Toddler Curriculum)*. Designed to be used as a pre-service model, an in-service model, or as an annual training plan to guarantee well-prepared and trained infant and toddler teachers who plan and implement developmentally appropriate infant and toddler curriculum. 308 pages.

ISBN 0-87659-260-4 / Gryphon House / 15826 / PB / $29.95

Available at your favorite bookstore, school supply store, or order directly from
Gryphon House at 800.638.0928 or www.gryphon house.com